MANAGE YOUR MONEY
LIKE A GROWNUP

The Best Money Advice
For Teens

SAM BECKBESSINGER

MANAGE
YOUR
MONEY

LIKE A
GROWNUP

THE BEST
MONEY ADVICE FOR
TEENS

Jonathan Ball Publishers

Johannesburg • Cape Town • London

Originally published in South Africa in 2020 by
JONATHAN BALL PUBLISHERS
A division of Media24 (Pty) Ltd
PO Box 33977
Jeppestown
2043

ISBN 978-1-77619-032-4
ebook ISBN 978-1-77619-033-1

*Every effort has been made to trace the copyright holders and to obtain
their permission for the use of copyright material. The publishers apologise
for any errors or omissions and would be grateful to be notified of
any corrections that should be incorporated in future editions of this book.*

Excerpt from Harry Potter and the Deathly Hallows *by JK Rowling
reproduced with permission from The Blair Partnership.*

Website: www.jonathanball.co.za
Twitter: www.twitter.com/JonathanBallPub
Facebook: www.facebook.com/JonathanBallPublishers

Cover by publicide
Design and typesetting by Nazli Jacobs
Illustrations by Nanna Venter
Set in ITC Veljovic

For my mum and dad,
who taught me about what really matters.

CONTENTS

DISCLAIMER

Okay, buddies, let's get some stuff straight so me and my nice publishers don't get sued.

Things change in the money space all the time. When I talk about how certain asset types (like property or shares) have grown in the past, that's no guarantee that they will continue to do so in the future. The world might change and that might make some things in this book incorrect, if you read it in the future. Also, the whole world's economy might collapse any day now (thanks, Boomers) and the oceans may rise and we might move to an entirely tinned-goods and drinkable-water-based economy, in which case I have no idea what you should invest in. But the principles you'll learn – earning, saving, investing – will probably hold up in most situations.

All money is in South African rands unless I say otherwise. I assume 8% per year real investment growth (growth after inflation). That's about what South African shares did between 2000 and 2016. Obviously, your own returns might not be 8%.

Neither the author nor the publisher may be held responsible for any action or claim resulting from the use of this book. Also, always wipe front to back.

PART 1

UNDERSTANDING

MONEY

Chapter 1

THIS BOOK IS FOR YOU

YOUR DREAMS MATTER

This book is about freedom. Yes, yes, I know it says on the cover that it's about money, but that's just a decoy to bamboozle the adults. (Did it work? In my experience, adults are EASILY BAMBOOZLED.) Really, what I want to talk to you about is how to live the life you actually want to live, not the life that the world wants to force you into.

I bet you have some big dreams for your life. Maybe something like one of these?

- Skateboarding, snowboarding and surfing your way through the wildest wild places on earth
- Making art, or music, or movies that people talk about for years
- Saving the world through work or activism that improves the fate of people, animals and the planet
- Buying a parent/guardian the house they've always wanted, so they can live in the comfort they deserve
- Becoming a sports star or athlete at the top of their game
- Having a huge circle of friends who go on adventures together all around the world
- Being a celebrity Twitch streamer or YouTuber who gets to share their obsessions with their fans
- Having a big family and lots of time to spend with them
- Inventing something or starting a company that solves one of the world's big problems

- Becoming a master chef and wowing the world with your delicious creations
- Studying all sorts of different things that interest you
- Living a humble life in nature without stress or worry.

Now let me ask you a question: how many of the adults you know seem to be living the lives that they dreamt of when they were your age? Or rather, how many of them seem to hate their jobs? Have you ever thought about why that happens: why so many kids with big dreams grow up into adults who feel trapped?

The reality is, anything you want to do with your life costs money. It costs money to support the people you care about. It costs money to have enough free time to practise the sport or art you love until you get good at it. It costs money to start a business or go on adventures or buy a surfboard. It also costs money to do more basic things like buy food to stay alive!

If you don't work out how to control your money, you end up spending your whole adult life just trying to make money and never actually enjoying the life you are living. Money ends up controlling you.

Have you ever started dreaming about what you want your life to look like, only to find yourself feeling a bit unsure about it all? Your dreams are just great – you start feeling yourself rise and rise like you are on a hot-air balloon ride over a game park, drifting into the sunset – BUT then when you think about how to make this all happen, you're suddenly back on Earth (with a bump)?

This book's about how to keep the gas turned on, and the hot-air balloon rising.

The better you understand how money works, the more you can use it as a tool to get the life you really want. When you're not in control of money, any money that comes into your life leaves it very quickly, which means that you have to spend a lot of time thinking about how to earn more of it, every day. The funny thing is that the best way to NOT have to think about money a lot is to understand it very well. Understanding money means you don't have to stress about it, so you can rather think about more fun things.[1]

So, this book is for you, even if you don't care about getting rich. This book is about how to better your chances of living the life YOU want to live, rather than just having to do any job that will pay you money. This book is for you if you've ever worried that there might be a bit of a gap between your future dreams and being 'practical'. And, if you've decided not to think about money/growing up/ saving because it all looks a bit boring, and you'd rather be having fun, this book is for you too.

Because really, this isn't a book about money at all. It's a book about freedom.

Have a chat with your parents or guardians about their jobs. What did they dream of becoming when they grew up? What do they like about their jobs now? What don't they like? How did they end up doing what they do?

OH, HELLO!

But wait! How rude of me. Let me introduce myself: my name's Sam. And this is my cat, Digby. Digby doesn't know

---

[1] Like, if you invented time travel and went back 200 years, how would you convince them that you ARE from the future without getting burned as a witch?

much about money because he pays rent in furballs. But he's cute, anyway, so I told him he could help write this book.

When I was a kid, the thing I really wanted to do with my life was write books, because I love books more than anything (okay, fine, except Digby). But there was just one problem: I had no idea how to go about actually doing that! Writing books isn't a job that someone will give you and pay you a salary to do. And I was REALLY BAD at managing money (but very good at spending it) so I ended up spending my 20s doing a bunch of really weird jobs, including dressing up like the Easter Bunny, handing out pamphlets at robots and writing letters on behalf of Ronald McDonald (no, really).[2] Eventually I realised that no one was going to give me the job I wanted, so I was going to have to invent it for myself – which meant figuring out how money works.

---

2   For real! Every town has real people whose full-time job it is to do public appearances as Ronald. They're trained in clown skills and they go to a big convention in America every year called RonCon.

So, I went and learnt everything I could learn about money. I even got myself a job in the finance industry so that I could learn about it from the inside. And I learnt a SHOCKING SECRET . . . dun dun duuuuun . . . money is actually really easy to understand!

I was really irritated when I learnt this, because I thought, *Why did no one teach me how money works when I was young, so that I could be much further ahead by now?* Because it really IS simple. You'll see.

Ever since then I've made it my mission to share this secret with everyone I know. My friends started avoiding me because I just wanted to tell them about money all the time. So that's why I'm turning to you, a fresh new audience to pelt with money facts!

Only joking.

Seriously.

But also, I wrote this book because I want you to get a head start and not have to spend your 20s pretending to be a fast-food mascot like I did.

I wrote this book especially for kids up to about 14, because if you're older than that you can probably just read the other book I wrote for adults (it has much more swearing in it, sorry! I need my mouth washed out with soap). But if you're reading this at 18 or 48, no problem. I read kids' books too! (John Green is pretty much my favourite writer and I will FIGHT anyone who says a bad thing about him.) Just enjoy. You'll be able to skip some of the chapters when you DO read my other book. Or maybe you're one of those really precocious six-year-olds like the ones from *MasterChef*, in which case, hello to you too!

Whoever you are, I'm really glad you're here. And I hope we can be friends.

TOO YOUNG? SAYS WHO?!

This book gives you the nuts-and-bolts low-down on one of the things that dominate most people's lives: money. Because believe me, it can dominate lives, no matter what kind of family you're from.

Maybe your family seems to have a lot of it, and there's no stress and it seems like there's a solid plan. Maybe your family struggles a bit, but holds it together. Maybe it seems like quite a big problem, one you'd rather not know anything about. Just another one of those adult problems that seems a lifetime away.

Right?

Wrong.

You know you're young. I know you're young. But I promise you, this is stuff you want to know now.

Here's why.

a) Good habits

The ideas and habits that you pick up at this stage in your life will shape you forever. Sure, you're probably not going to earn HUGE amounts of cash in your teen years (unless you're a kid celebrity or something), but it's still the best time to learn how to earn, spend and save money well. The good habits you need to manage a R100 birthday present today are the same habits that you'll need to manage the R1 million you'll earn one day.[3] It's like practising any sport or spending time on any passion – the hours you put in now will lay the foundation for success later.

It's like how people who grow up to be amazing athletes or artists start training when they're young. Serena Williams,

---

3   Probably even more than R1 million, actually. We'll get to that in a minute.

the best tennis player in the world, started training when she was three years old. She said:

> When I was a kid I trained really, really, really hard. And I think that's so important for kids out there that want to grow up and be the best. Ask any professional player. You train really hard. You train for hours. I remember in the summer, we would train from, I think it was from like 9:00 to 11:00 and then 1:00 to 6:00. And then on Saturdays, we would train from 9:00 to 12:00. And then we would have Sundays off. So we trained a lot. We practised hours and hours and hours. And obviously when you get older, you don't practise as much, but you're building a really strong foundation when you're younger so you can have a solid foundation that doesn't shake when you get old.

b) The best time to make mistakes

In Chapter 6 we'll be looking at how developing your entrepreneurial skills (aka your side-hustle) can bring you in some extra cash. One of the key things entrepreneurs say about starting a business as a kid is that it gives you the chance to make lots of mistakes while you still have the safety net of your home and family looking after you and supporting you (and you don't have to worry about buying food for your idiot cat). It's an idea you can apply to all of this money information – that the best time to start learning is now – because the best learning often happens when you make mistakes. And NOW is the time to make mistakes, my friends!

c) Your chance to prove everyone wrong

Some people say kids are pretty bad at understanding the value of delayed gratification. In other words, put a marshmallow in front of a child (or a 33-year-old woman named Sam), and tell them that if they can resist eating the marshmallow for ten minutes, they can have two marshmallows. The general consensus is: many of those children or Sams will eat the marshmallow now, because they think that one marshmallow now is worth twice as much as a hypothetical future marshmallow (you can watch videos of this experiment on YouTube, if you like watching kids give in to temptation).

This is where you need to prove everyone wrong. Delaying gratification is something you're going to have to learn to do. But it's going to be easy for you. Because you're going to LOVE saving those marshmallows, and watching them grow into more marshmallow babies. Promise.

d) Money loves time

Warren Buffett is the fourth richest person in the world (he has about $88 billion,[4] and he's working on giving 99% of it away to charity). He didn't get rich by inventing something or robbing a bank, but because he was really good at investing money. Warren Buffett tells everyone that the most important trick to investing is patience, because of a magical thing called compound interest (which you'll learn about in Chapter 3), so the best way to invest is to start as early as possible. He should know: he started investing when he was 11 years old.

---

4   Yes, BILLION. With a 'B'!

MONEY IS A RESPONSIBILITY

The other reason that it's really important to learn how to manage money is that you're probably going to have to manage a LOT of it over your lifetime.

We think of millionaires as being people who've really made it. But most of us will earn a lot more than a million rand over our lifetimes. If you start working at age 20 and you work until you're 65, that means you'll be working for **45 years**. That's nearly half a century! This means that even if you don't earn a very big salary, you're still earning a lot of money over your whole lifetime.

WHAT DIFFERENT CAREERS CAN EARN			
Career	Monthly salary	Yearly salary	Lifetime salary
Cashier	R3 500	R42 000	R1 890 000
Teacher	R15 000	R180 000	R8 100 000
Doctor	R50 000	R600 000	R27 000 000
Lawyer	R110 000	R1 320 000	R59 400 000

These are just averages I got from Google. Some people earn much more or much less than these numbers.

Looking after all that money is a lot of responsibility! There's so much you could do with it. You could use it to make life better for yourself, the people you love and the world around you. That money could be happiness fuel. But if you don't learn how to manage it well, that money won't make ANYONE happy, and wouldn't that be a waste?

WHAT THIS BOOK WILL COVER

This book is broken up into three parts: **understanding money**, **making money** and **managing money**.

The sooner you start to figure out how money and you fit together in this world, the sooner you'll be able to feel comfortable about a whole lot of things that go along with money. So, **Part 1** is a crash course about how money works. We'll cover:

- **In Chapter 2:** Why different families have such different experiences with money, and why your folks might have more or less money to spend on you than your friends' folks.
- **In Chapter 3:** How people get wealthy. We'll spend a lot of time in this chapter talking about the weirdest and most magical thing money does (compound interest).
- **In Chapter 4:** Understanding the systems that make some people poor, and thinking about where you fit into the bigger picture.

You can't practise managing money until you've got some, so **Part 2** is all about making that dough. We'll talk about:

- **In Chapter 5:** The pros and cons of getting an allowance, and how to understand your folks' reasons for giving you the amount of money that they do.
- **In Chapter 6:** What you can do to make yourself more money, including learning how to be a ~~CRIMINAL MASTERMIND~~ genius kid entrepreneur.
- **In Chapter 7:** How to start thinking about the type of career you want to have one day.

In **Part 3**, we get practical and talk about the basics of spending and saving. We'll cover:

- **In Chapter 8:** Setting up a system that directs your money to where you want it to go.
- **In Chapter 9:** Saving for the things you REALLY want (maybe a Switch? iPad? Robot giraffe?) and how to start investing.

- **In Chapter 10:** Outwitting advertisers and being a savvier spender. How to avoid that feeling you get after spending your allowance on the perfect pair of jeans (the jeans that don't seem so perfect any more once you get home).
- **In Chapter 11:** Using your money as a force for good in the world, including giving to charity and being an ethical consumer.

There's a website that goes along with this book, at manageyourmoneylikeagrownup.com. On it, you'll find tools, tips and useful things to download (plus, you can see what Digby looks like in real life).

IN SUMMARY!

- Understanding how money works is one of the best ways you can make sure you live the life YOU really want to live.
- You're not too young to start earning, saving and investing your money. In fact, now's the best time to learn good habits and take big risks.

You ready? Let's go!

Chapter 2

MONEY AND YOUR FAMILY

MY FAMILY AND OTHER ANIMALS

My home growing up was basically a zoo. My mum is one of those warmhearted people who just loves to rescue animals. Once, we had a dog that went missing, and my mum went to the SPCA to try to find it, and she came home with ELEVEN DOGS because they all needed homes.[5] And we didn't just have dogs: we had cats, horses, budgies, quails, hamsters, a donkey named Mr Magoo, a pet pig named Petunia who slept in the kitchen, goats and pet marmoset monkeys (one of which, I kid you not, I was named after). It was chaos, but the good kind of chaos that's filled with love.

All of these animals were expensive to look after, and sometimes my parents got very stressed out about money. But getting rid of the animals was never an option, because they were our family.

Every family is different, and that's wonderful! There's no right or wrong way for a family to be. And every family has its own **culture**. By culture I mean 'the way things are done around here', the rules that you live by. This extends to money, too.

The funny thing about culture is that often it's invisible to the people who grew up in that culture. Here's an example:

---

5   We had to ban my mum from going to the SPCA because we did not have any more room in our house for more dogs.

did you know that people in some parts of the world think it's really, really weird and gross to wipe your butt with toilet paper? After they poop, they clean themselves with water. Now, if you grew up wiping your butt with TP you just think it's a very normal thing and you probably never think about it, but it's actually just a part of our culture, and it's worth remembering that not everyone does things the same way.

So, in this chapter, you're going to try to take a step back and examine your family's money culture. Understanding your family's money culture will help you to figure out what the rules are for money in your own family, and how you can use rules best. It will also help you to understand how your family might be different from other families, and why.

When you do this, it might help to imagine that you're an alien and you're studying humans for the first time, like an explorer. It's really important that we're not trying to **judge** our family's money culture, we're just trying to understand it.

Because, it's not only you who is special and unique. Surprise! Your parents, or guardians, are special and unique

too.[6] They've decided to bring you up in their own unique and special way. Lucky you! This means that they have their own money culture and THEIR rules are in play. Love

---

6   Generally, in this book, I'm going to refer to the adults in your family as your 'folks', because not everyone lives with their parents.

them or hate them, it's part of what makes you who you are. Remember this when you're talking to them about things like pocket money, allowances and whether you get paid to do chores.

At some point (hopefully), your folks made some decisions about how to split the work involved in looking after you, and how to share the cost of looking after you. You might know what financial arrangements there are in your family to support you, or you might not, depending on what your folks want to share with you. But the arrangements are there.

Families are usually money teams. They all work together for shared goals, and they all look after one another. Some families like individual family members to each have their OWN money, and share costs fairly. Other families like to think of all the money in the family as belonging to everyone equally. There's no right or wrong way, but it can be helpful for you to understand how your family thinks about this.

By the way, in some families, some adults don't work for money, but instead do unpaid work taking care of the family. A lot of the work that needs to be done in a society isn't paid for (stuff like cooking and cleaning and looking after children and the elderly),[7] but this unpaid work is just as important and valuable as paid work.

> Remember: your value as a person, and other people's value as people, is unconnected to how much you or they earn. A strange thing about work is that the true value of work (in the sense of what's really important in the world) is not connected to how much you get paid for it. Business-people often get paid more money than doctors do, and doctors literally save lives!

Families have lots of different arrangements about who works for money, who pays for things, and who does other kinds of

---

[7] In the olden days, it was almost always women who did this work for free, while men did work that earned money. It can make you very vulnerable to not earn your own money. Did you know that women couldn't have their own credit cards until the 1970s?

unpaid work. Sometimes this gets extra complicated where there are **blended families** with children from different parents, or extended family like cousins and grandparents that you support too, or where one of your parents doesn't live with you. A big part of being an adult is figuring out how to create a family where how work and money are split feels fair and makes everyone happy. One day, you're going to have the chance to create your own kind of family.

THE STORIES YOU PICK UP

My main reason for wanting to write about money for kids was that, in my own family, we never spoke about money when I was growing up. In my house, you could make jokes about sex at the dinner table, you could have a robust and respectful discussion about politics or religion, but I do not remember a single conversation we ever had as a family about how money works, or our family's financial situation. Ever.

Money was the final taboo.

But the thing is, even while my parents weren't talking to me about money, that didn't mean I wasn't doing my best to work out what was going on. Like all kids, I was a sponge, sucking up information. Maybe you're like me, and you've heard the anxious fights your parents have behind closed doors. As a child, I could sense when they were stressed about covering the bills.

Turns out, the whole time my parents were avoiding the topic I was learning some fundamental beliefs about money – beliefs that it took me a really long time to unlearn.

Money stories – the ideas you have about money – are a part of your family money culture. There is a researcher named Brad Klontz who studies money beliefs. He groups the ideas we hold about money into four basic groups:

1. **Money avoidance.** 'Rich people are greedy.' 'People get rich by taking advantage of others.' 'It's not okay to have more than you need.' 'I don't deserve a lot of money when other people have less than me.'
2. **Money worship.** 'More money will make you happier.' 'There will never be enough money.' 'Money is power.' 'Things would get better if I had more money.' 'I will never be able to afford the things I really want in life.'
3. **Money status.** 'Your self-worth equals your net worth.' 'I won't buy something unless it's new.' 'If you live a good life, you'll always have enough money.' 'Most poor people don't deserve to have money.'
4. **Money vigilance.** 'It's important to save for a rainy day.' 'If you can't pay cash for something, you shouldn't buy it.' 'Money should be saved, not spent.' 'You shouldn't tell people how much you have or make.'

Which of these money stories are true? All of them, probably, even the ones that contradict each other. All of them capture part of the truth. But none of them is the whole truth. And some of them are more helpful to you, at particular times in your life, than others.

My mum, who grew up quite poor, carries a lot of the 'money worship' beliefs, because she's always feared not having enough money. I think many people who grow up poor end up believing that money will fix all your problems, so if you have problems, it's because you don't have enough money.

The thing is, this belief was definitely true during some parts of her life when she really did not have enough money. But it still felt true to her during times when she had plenty –

times when the things that were wrong in her life had nothing to do with money at all. Even when she actually had plenty of money, my mum was constantly talking about what she was going to do when she won the Lotto. She always had a strong sense of the things she couldn't afford, the life she could have been living but wasn't.

For my dad, money was about status, and it was how he demonstrated his love. If my dad had R5 left in his bank account, he would spend that last R5 buying you ice cream. Money moved through his life like water. If he had it, he'd spend it without thinking, and mostly, he'd spend it on other people. If you mentioned that you kinda half-liked a bizarre overpriced hat you saw in a store window, he would march out immediately and buy you that hat, whether you actually had any use for it or not. If he didn't have the cash, he'd buy it with a credit card.

Money was always like a happy surprise, to my dad. Like, 'Oh look, money! What a strange and fun thing to find in my bank account! Let's go spend it, quick, before it vanishes as mysteriously as it arrived!'

Both of them were amazing parents who loved their kids. And both of their money philosophies kind of made sense but were also kind of insane.

You can imagine how hilarious my parents were together, with their very different money beliefs. My mum would literally hide money from my dad. And thank goodness, too, because my mum was the only one thinking about how we were going to pay for less exciting magical goodies like school fees (and my dad's big credit-card bills). But she'd also take us to one side tearfully every single year and warn us that they couldn't afford to buy us proper Christmas presents that year (which was nuts: we always had way-over-the-top Christmas presents, but she never felt like it was enough, and was always convinced that we were on the edge of financial disaster). It was a confusing time.

I, a dumb kid, concluded two completely opposite facts about my family's financial situation from my parents' different behaviour:

1. We did not have enough money!
2. We had plenty of money!

And because my parents never actually had a conversation with me about any of this, I never had a chance to reflect on questions like what it would mean to have enough money, how you go about getting money in the first place, and how to make decisions about how to spend the money you do have. In this information vacuum, I started forming some beliefs about money:

- You have no control over how much money you have.
- Money is mysterious and it's impossible to know whether you have enough or not.
- It's weird and wrong to ever talk about money (I'm making up for this now by talking about money ALL THE TIME AT VERY INAPPROPRIATE MOMENTS).

My dear, sweet parents, who wanted nothing but the best for us, did all they could to protect us from money conversations. But when I think about it, the money stories that I picked up are so peculiar that it took me a long, long time to unpick these ideas from my brain, and replace them with more helpful beliefs that don't leave me feeling so confused. So I really want to get you to think about money BEFORE the ideas you pick up get you into trouble.

I now know:

- Anyone with the advantages you have – I'm assuming you are getting a good education and have access to books – can work out a plan to control money so that it doesn't control you.
- There are no mysteries to money. Yes, there are certain tricks to making money grow in a way that seems magical – and yes, I'm going to teach them to you. But money is not a mystery, just something that not everyone knows enough about. The only mysterious money is leprechaun money.
- There's nothing shameful about talking about money, whether you have a lot of it or a little.

Which money stories have you picked up from your family? Which of the four types of money stories do YOU think is more true?

YOUR FAMILY MONEY CULTURE

Some of the ways families are different:
- Heaps of pocket money
- No allowance or irregular allowance
- Very organised regular allowance
- You get told what you are expected to use your allowance on
- You get paid for doing chores
- Everyone is expected to do chores for free
- There aren't chores because a domestic worker is paid to do everything
- Children have bank accounts
- Children get money as birthday presents
- Your folks will buy you anything you ask for
- Your folks encourage you to save for what you want
- Children have jobs.

There will be a lot of reasons why your family has the money culture it has. Maybe your family doesn't give you an allowance because they can't afford it, or maybe they're trying to teach you something. Even in many rich families, children don't get lots of pocket money. Often, parents feel that children need to learn to make their own money, or learn to manage the money they have, rather than just getting what they ask for.

Remember, you're pretending to be an alien explorer, just trying to understand your family, not judging!

FAMILY INCOME

At this point in your life, you (probably) get your money from your family, but how do THEY get money? You might know all this, but if any of this brings up something you don't already know – like what your folks do for a living – then it's probably time to get them to open up.[8]

There are lots of different ways for families to earn money:

- **Salary:** Money that someone else pays them monthly, for doing a job. If someone gets paid daily or weekly, they might call this **wages**, but it means the same thing.
- **Own business:** Someone in your family might be an entrepreneur, which means that they have their own business. Sometimes, they'll work in the business and pay themselves a salary, but if the business makes a profit they get to keep that too.

---

8   If your parents start looking edgy if you ask them what their jobs are, they are definitely undercover spies and you should get them to teach you how to crack codes.

- **Lump sums:** Some people do the kind of work that means they don't get paid monthly – they might get paid after finishing a big project, or after making a major sale if they are selling their own work (an artist after an exhibition, for example).
- **Royalties:** Money you get for something you made or invented. If your father wrote a best-selling novel and your mother invented and patented a New Age solar-powered battery, they might get paid lump sums every year.
- **Pensions:** Your grandparents may be getting their money from a pension, which is a kind of long-term savings account that they paid into while they were earning. Your parents are probably saving into their own pension fund too, as a way of making sure there's money for them when they're older.
- **Investments:** Money you earn from stuff you own, like if your family has a shed in the back yard that people rent out, or if you own shares. We'll talk about other types of investments in Chapter 9.
- **Social grants:** Money from the government to support people who have extra needs. In South Africa, the main people who get grants are people who are responsible for children, older people and people living with disabilities, if they need extra money.
- **Family support:** Many people get money from other family members or people they care about. Where parents don't live together and one parent looks after the children most of the time, the other parent will sometimes pay child support, for example.
- **Inheritance:** This is inherited money, or property that gets passed down from one generation to the next, when

someone dies. In South Africa, it's also often called inter-generational wealth.

Generally, there are two main types of income:

1. **Active income:** Money earned from *work you've done.* Salaries and wages are active income.
2. **Passive income:** Money from *stuff you own.* Royalties, profit from a business you own, and investments are passive income. This money is awesome because you can be super-lazy and still earn money.

Generally, the richer people are, the more their money comes from **passive income** rather than from **active income**. Figuring out how to build up **passive income** is one of the best ways to live a freer life.

HOW DO PEOPLE INHERIT PROPERTY OR MONEY?

Remember Harry Potter visiting the vault at Gringotts and discovering the pile of gold that his parents left him? That was inherited wealth.

Usually, when a person dies, they leave a will saying who in the family will inherit what. Some of it is sentimental – like your granny's wedding ring, a beautiful tea set, even a Bentley or a Rolls, or just the family photos. Some of it might be property, and some of it may be money. Sometimes money is put into something called a trust fund, which manages family investments.

It's important to know that most people do not have inherited wealth. Some people inherit a whole lot; most people inherit nothing. The world's unfair like that.

Choose five to seven questions from the list below that you'd like to ask your folks. Write these questions on a piece of paper and then, every night for a week, hand over the question of the night to whichever adult you are putting in the hot seat! If you prefer, add your own questions to the list.

Before you start, agree on some rules about how these conversations are going to go. Remember to approach these chats like an alien explorer! Here are some suggestions for how to talk about money with your folks:

1. Be polite and ask them if they are happy to discuss the question you have selected. If not, they can move on to another.
2. Give them time to explain themselves.
3. Your folks don't have to tell you how much they earn or how much they have saved, unless they choose to.

SOME QUESTIONS FOR YOUR FOLKS

1. Did you have money growing up?
2. How do you earn your money?
3. How did you get the job you have now?
4. Do you think money is evil or good? Why?
5. Do you ever get stressed about money?
6. What did YOUR parents teach you about money?
7. What is the best money decision you have ever made?
8. Are you saving for me to study after school?
9. Do you think people should talk about money more?
10. Do you think it's okay for kids to know how much their parents earn?

FAMILY EXPENSES

Your family will have expenses – money that gets paid out for things you all need. Every family's expenses are different. Yours might include stuff like this:

- Groceries
- Electricity and water
- Paying rent or a home loan
- School fees
- Transport
- Pocket money/allowances for kids
- Medical aid
- Pets (donkeys, monkeys, 11 dogs ...)
- Insurance
- Tithing/giving money to charity
- Salaries for a domestic worker
- Holidays
- Fixing stuff that breaks around the house
- Going out/having adventures
- Buying fun things like games/books/gadgets
- Saving for retirement

TOYS FOR DIGBY [9]

See what you and your folks can add to the list above!

---

9   Hey, how did that get there?

Obviously, families need to make sure that they are not spending more on their expenses than they are getting in as income. They need to balance their **cash flow**.

> Cash flow is made up of two things: money coming in (income) and money going out (expenses).

Balancing your cash flow means making sure that your expenses aren't bigger than your income, so you don't run out of money.

Did you notice that you feature on the list of expenses? Having children can be expensive. Being a responsible adult means NOT giving your children more than you can afford.

There's another thing that might be in your family budget. Sometimes a lot of family income can go to supporting others. Because of history and culture, many black South Africans are supporting not just aging parents, but also extended family, siblings and family friends. It's sometimes called *ubuntu* tax or black tax (although it can happen to anyone). It isn't a horrible thing! We love our families and it can be a privilege to help look after their well-being. But, when added to the other unfairnesses faced by black people, this can make it very hard for families to balance their cash flow, much less save and build up wealth. We'll talk more about inequalities like this in Chapter 4.

In fact, quite a lot of families, even rich ones, struggle with balancing cash flow, and actually this is one of those money conversations my parents never had with me. But we're doing things differently here!

Some families balance their cash flow by making a budget. That's where you list all of your expenses, work out how much they cost every month and make sure that they're less than your income.

Practise your budgeting skills by drawing up a monthly budget for a pet. Do this for your actual pets, or for your pretend one.[10] Do some research and get the actual prices for stuff online (or ask your folks to take you to a shop). You may need to find out your pet's weight (or the ideal weight of your pretend pet) as the amount of food they need is usually worked out based on weight.[11] Remember to add things like cat litter for cats.

Here's an example, based on my friend Angela's Dalmatian, Boogle.

Boogle has allergies, so he needs anti-itch gels sometimes. He weighs 30 kg.

- Flea and tick meds: R520 for three months divided by 3 = R170
- 2 × 10 kg bags of dog food at R400 each = R800
- 10 bones a month at R10 each = R100
- Anti-itch gel = R200
- Boogle goes to the vet about four times a year at R300 a visit, so R1 200 a year. That averages out to R100 a month.

Monthly budget for one medium-sized dog = R1 370

What even IS money?

Years ago, before money, people traded stuff. Some stuff was more valuable than others – let's say ten chickens = one goat, for example. People ended up in debt to one another in complicated ways ('Last winter, Grawrg gave

---

10 I'd love to see a budget for a pet dragon.
11 This is why you should never buy a horse.

me a goat, and I've given her back 20 eggs, so I probably still owe her a lot of eggs'), and people had to invent writing just to keep track of all of it (thanks, Sumerians!).

Eventually, people realised that they could use tokens to represent value, so rather than just saying, 'Hey, I owe you for that goat you gave me,' you could get specific: 'I owe you 100 tokens for that goat you gave me.' As you know from playing board games, you can use anything to represent value, as long as you all agree on what the value of that thing is. In different parts of the world, people used shells, bones and beads to act as early tokens of value. That was the first money.

As people started mining and working with metals like gold and silver, they started using those as money. Bars of gold, or gold or silver coins, came to be used. But the problem there was that they were heavy to carry around. Gradually, people started leaving their ACTUAL gold or silver with bankers or goldsmiths, in exchange for bits of paper that said how much gold they had left there. These notes started being used instead of the coins – and that's how the very first banknotes came into being.

After a while, governments started printing paper money, and coins made of less valuable metal like copper were produced. The paper and metal that the notes and coins are made of are not in themselves valuable, but they have the value that is printed on them. The government that prints the money guarantees that there is value in the money. (So, fun fact, it's actually illegal to burn or destroy money.)

For a long time, South Africa actually kept piles of gold bars in a vault to guarantee the money. But that is no longer the case.

South African money is printed at the Reserve Bank in Pretoria. It is obviously very important that only the government prints money, otherwise the guarantee that there is value in the money would be false. Fake money is called counterfeit money. The Reserve Bank has certain markers on the notes that people who handle a lot of notes (like bank tellers and shopkeepers) can use to tell whether the money is fake.

Some things to check on your moolah:
- Does it have a watermark that you can see when you hold it up to the light?
- Do the lines on the front of the note stand out (are they ridged)?
- Is the number on the left side the same as the number on the top right?
- If you move a real banknote, the big number on the right bottom corner changes colour – it shines.

IN SUMMARY!

- You and your money are part of a family economy. Every family money culture is unique.
- You pick up a lot of ideas about money from your family. These ideas or 'money stories' can either help you, or become problems. So it's useful to think about what they are.
- Your parents will only give you what they can afford to – that's called being responsible.
- **Expenses** are money going out; **income** is money coming in.
- Learning to manage money will help you manage your **cash flow** (making sure you're not spending more than you earn).

Chapter 3
THE MAGIC OF COMPOUND INTEREST

MAGIC MONEY

> 'Your mother can't produce food out of thin air,' said Hermione. 'No one can. Food is the first of the five Principal Exceptions to Gamp's Law of Elemental Transfigur—'
>
> 'Oh, speak English, can't you?' Ron said, prising a fish bone out from between his teeth.
>
> 'It's impossible to make good food out of nothing! You can Summon it if you know where it is, you can transform it, you can increase the quantity if you've already got some—'
>
> 'Well, don't bother increasing this, it's disgusting,' said Ron.[12]

My favourite parts of *Harry Potter* are the parts where they're in class, understanding how a new piece of magic works (yes, I'm such a nerd that I even like READING about school; don't judge me, okay?). I like books where the magic has rules and logic: it can do amazing things, but you have to understand how it works. You can't just wiggle your wand and hope for pancakes.

Well, it turns out that money is a special kind of magic,

---

12 *Harry Potter and the Deathly Hallows*, J.K. Rowling.

and it has rules too. And you have to understand those rules if you want it to do anything cool for you.

There's one rule of money that's more powerful than any of the others. If you understand this rule, really, properly understand it, you'll already be better at money than most grownups. It's a bit of magic called **compound interest**. You might not have heard of those words before, so let's take them one by one.

INTEREST

Interest is the cost of using someone else's money. Let's say you really, *reeeeally* want to buy a robot tiger that costs R1 000, but you can't afford it. So you go to borrow money from the bank. The bank will make you pay back the R1 000, but they will also make you pay a little bit extra. It's like a fee you were paying to 'rent' the R1 000 from the bank. That extra cost is the interest.[13]

The nifty thing about interest is that YOU can also be the one earning it. If you lend someone else money, they'll pay you interest.

You can even earn interest by lending your money to the bank! Now, you might be thinking, surely the bank has plenty of money – why would they borrow money from little old me? But you'd be wrong! Every time you put money into a savings account at the bank, that's actually what you're doing: lending them cash. The money you put in a savings account

---

13 This is why the Bank of Mom and Dad is so great: they normally don't charge any interest :)

at a bank isn't actually sitting in a big vault somewhere with your name on it. The bank is using that money to do bank things (like lend it to OTHER people), which means that the bank pays you interest for the privilege of using your dough.

More generally, in the world of money, we talk about 'interest' as being the money that you **earn** for investing your money or putting it to work in the world (good interest), or the **cost** of using someone else's money (bad interest).

Simple interest is calculated on the value of the amount you originally borrowed. Say you want to borrow R100 from the bank, and they say they will charge you 10% simple interest every year:

Year 1	10% of R100 = R10	So now you owe R100 + R10 = R110
Year 2	10% of R100 = R10	So now you owe R110 + R10 = R120
Year 3	10% of R100 = R10	So now you owe R120 + R10 = R130
Year 4	10% of R100 = R10	So now you owe R130 + R10 = R140
Year 5	10% of R100 = R10	So now you owe R140 + R10 = R150

So, after five years you'll pay back R150.

But **compound** interest is like supercharged HULK interest. It's not calculated on the original amount you borrowed, but on the **amount that's owed now**. So, if you borrow the same R100 with 10% compound interest, you'll pay it back like this:

Year 1	10% of R100 = R10	So now you owe R100 + R10 = R110
Year 2	10% of R110 = R11	So now you owe R110 + R11 = R121
Year 3	10% of R121 = R12	So now you owe R121 + R12 = R133
Year 4	10% of R133 = R13	So now you owe R133 + R13 = R146
Year 5	10% of R146 = R15	So now you owe R146 + R15 = R161

So, after five years you'll pay back R161. That R11 difference might not look like much, but it can make a huge difference when the amounts of money are much larger.

Almost everything in the world of money is worked out as compound interest, not simple interest.

If you study maths until matric, you'll be able to do complicated calculations involving compound interest on big sums of money. But the thing is, right now you don't need to understand the maths to understand how important it is. You just need to know what the maths does.

The thing you need to remember is that whenever a pile of money is accumulating interest that is compounded (which is how most interest works) it **grows crazy-fast**.

Here's a question for you. Would you rather I gave you a million rand cash, today, or gave you 1 cent that doubles every day for 30 days? I mean, they don't even make one-cent coins any more but let's imagine they did.

Sounds like a million rand would be the better way, right? Well, nope. If you take 1 cent and double it every day for a month, by the end of day 30 you'd have R5.3 million. From one tiny little cent.

Rats on a ship

Here's a story to help you understand compound interest, which I'm borrowing directly from my friend Georgina Armstrong because she explains it much better than I can.

Imagine there's a ship at the docks, getting ready to go on a long voyage, and two rats get on board.

For the sake of the example, there's one girl rat and one boy rat. Also, for the sake of this example, there are no cats on the ship.[14]

The ship sets sail, and the rats do what they do – they have babies. Pretty soon, there are more than two rats aboard. Then our original two rats continue to produce baby rats and the rat population on the boat steadily grows. With one pair of rats having babies on a regular basis (for simplicity, I'm saying that our rat pair can have two babies a month), it means that, if you draw a graph of rats over time, you get a nice straight line going up. This is how simple interest looks.

---

14 I'm sorry, Digby.

<u>9 MONTHS</u>
18 RATS

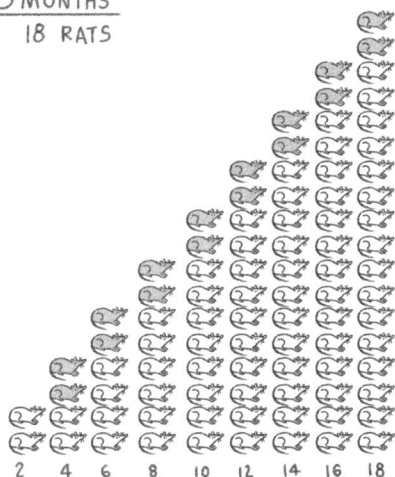

2 4 6 8 10 12 14 16 18

After nine months at sea, you have 18 rats on board. So far so good?

The thing is, you and I both know that rats are pretty gross and breed a lot faster than that. Let's be honest, as the months go by, it's not just going to be the original mommy rat and daddy rat having babies – the babies are going to start having babies. With each new month, yet another pair of baby rats is born and, one month after that, that pair produces their own pair of babies. So, the more the population of rats grows, the faster the population of rats grows, as babies produce babies who produce their own babies, and nobody stops having babies.

After nine months at sea, you have 512 rats on board, and there's not enough space in this picture to show them all.

By now, you probably regret not bringing a cat with you.

9 MONTHS
512 RATS

2 4 8 16 32 64 128 256 512

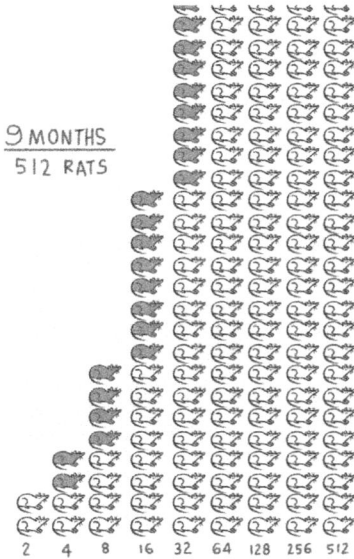

And, after 21 months at sea, you definitely regret the cat thing because you have 2 097 152 rats on board, and your ship sinks under the weight of 734 tons of rat. (Also, if we showed all those rats at this scale in this picture, and you printed the picture, it might be taller than the tallest building on earth.[15])

The absurd difference in growth between my first example (straight line) and my second example (curved line) is absolutely real. It's the difference between simple growth and compound growth. It's all growth, but it's compound growth that has the really powerful snowball effect.

---

15 Which, by the way, is a building in Dubai called the Burj Khalifa, which is so tall that you can see it from 100 km away. That would be like seeing the Drakensberg mountains from Durban.

21 MONTHS
2 097 152 RATS

How did vampires get so rich?

Let's talk about *Twilight* for a minute. (Don't look at me like that – yes, I love *Twilight*.) Or vampires in general, really. Have you noticed that vampires always live in fancy mansions and wear velvet waistcoats? And you know all that skin glitter ain't cheap.

How do they afford such extravagance?

Two hundred years ago, if a vampire had put R150 into a savings account that grows at just 8% a year, they'd have R1 billion right now. That buys a lot of velvet waistcoats.

Because that's the other thing you need to know about compound interest: the single most important factor involved is **time**. The longer you give your savings to grow, the better.

Now, you're probably not an immortal, blood-sucking demon (right? RIGHT?!) but time is still going to matter a lot to you in your financial life.

Let's imagine you start earning a salary when you're 25. Look at two scenarios:

1. You start saving R1 000 a month from your very first paycheque for retirement. You do that for just five years. At age 30, you stop saving and just leave your savings to do that magical compounding thing until you reach 65.

2. You start saving when you're 30. You save the same amount, a thousand bucks a month for five years, and you stop when you're 35.

Starting just five years later can't make that much of a difference, right?

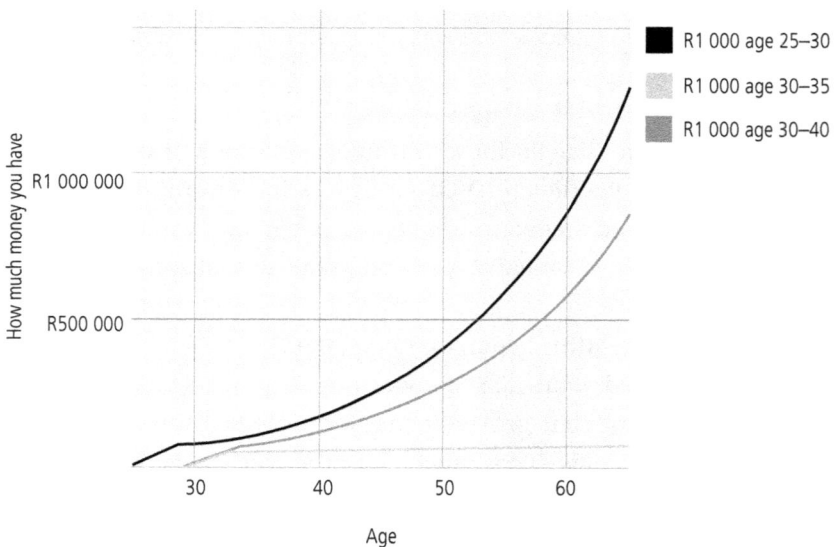

Ah, so, it turns out it makes a HUGE difference, actually. About a million bucks' worth of difference. In fact, to make up for lost time, the 30-year-old saver has to save for twice as long, or save an extra R500 every month, to catch up with the early saver.

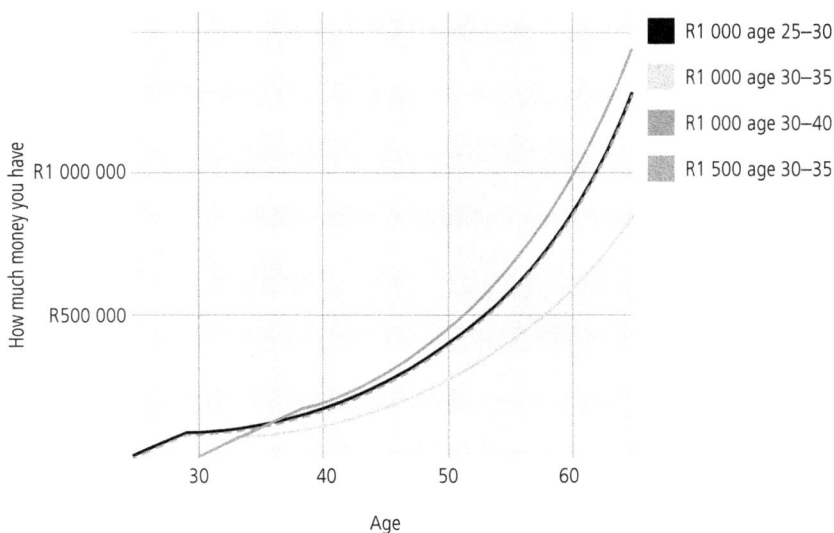

I want you to remember this: every year you wait to start saving, it costs you much more than you think it does. It doesn't just cost you the R5 000 or R10 000 you might save this year – it costs you the R220 000 or R450 000 that money will be worth in 40 years' time.

That's why you, reading this book now, have an opportunity that most people never have. Money loves time, and that's the thing you've got plenty of.

How debt compounds

We've mostly been talking about good compound interest, which is when you're the one EARNING it by saving or investing your money. But there's a dark side to this:[16] when you're the one PAYING the interest, it compounds too.

---

16 There's always a dark side. Ask Luke Skywalker.

Debt is money that you've borrowed from someone else, or from the bank (called a loan). You owe the money you borrowed, but you'll also need to pay interest on the loan. Nothing in this world comes for free.[17] Especially not when banks are involved.

There are different kinds of debt, and we'll cover them later. For now, you should just know about these two:

- **A loan:** When you borrow money for something big, like an iPad or a car or a house, and agree to pay it back over a specific time. When people borrow money to buy a house, it normally takes 20 years to pay it back!
- **Credit card:** A card linked to a bank account that lets you spend more money than you have, up to a limit. If you pay back the money, you are allowed to borrow that amount again, but the interest charged on credit cards is really high.

Most debt costs you interest. And because that interest is also COMPOUND interest, the time = money principle applies here too. Normally, the faster you pay back a debt, the less interest you pay.

Companies who lend money know this, and they use a bunch of sneaky tricks to encourage people to take as loooong as possible to pay back a debt, because that means more money for them. Mean, right?

DON'T BE A JOB SLAVE

Imagine that you are part of a family, Family A. Your family has some pet snorgles. Oh, you've never heard of snorgles?

---

17 Except sunshine and cuddles from cats.

They are 100% ABSOLUTELY REAL CREATURES and this is what they look like.[18]

These little creatures are adorable and they make everyone happy, but each snorgle needs to eat an apple every day to survive. You've got to go out and pick a bunch of apples every day to feed the snorgles. In this analogy, apples are your income and snorgles are your expenses. Your job is going to your neighbour's apple field and picking apples.

At the end of every month, you have no apples left, because you fed all of them to your snorgles. In your real family, this would be what happens if every cent of income is spent on stuff like food and school fees.

When you spend everything that you earn, your money is flowing like this:

INCOME   EXPENSES

---

18   No, snorgles don't really exist outside of my very active imagination.

But there is a problem with this picture. Someone who feeds all their apples to their snorgles every month is always one paycheque or disaster away from being flat broke. Even if they earn a lot of money every month, they don't have freedom. They are what I call a job slave.

Why? Well, every decision they make is dictated by money. Every month, they're living from paycheque to paycheque. A job slave can't decide to quit their job suddenly if they get treated badly. A job slave can't do any of those things you want to do – take a few years off to study further, or to volunteer for the organisation they feel is going to save the world.

The problem is that paycheques are not completely in your control. Eventually, any job slave will hit a problem. You might lose your job suddenly, get sick and be unable to work, or have some huge, unexpected expenses.

So, imagine that you had a big expense you didn't see coming (one of your snorgles ate a bee and there were vet bills), or you're sick and you can't pick apples for a while. You have no savings, so you have to go and borrow apples from your creepy neighbour Murta. This is debt. Sometime, you'll have to give back to Murta the money that you owe her. But because she's doing you a favour, Murta says you also have to adopt her really gross pet, the Interest Monster, and feed him too.

But Murta's **Interest Monster grows much faster than snorgles**. The longer it takes you to pay back Murta, the bigger he gets, and the more apples he eats every day. Take too long to pay back Murta, and you'll find yourself spending all your money trying to keep the Interest Monster in apples, until you don't have enough left to feed your own snorgles. This is a debt spiral.

For many people, this gets so bad that 70–80% of every pay-cheque first has to feed the Interest Monster before you can buy anything else. It means you can never buy new stuff, because you're still paying for stuff you bought in the past.

The truth is that lots of families in South Africa live in a debt spiral, for lots of reasons (often, people just weren't earning enough money to begin with). Your family might be one of them. It might be one of the reasons why they can't afford to give you more pocket money. That's their business. The reason they have bought you this book is that they want you to do better. That's your business!

START THINKING ABOUT ASSETS

So far, we've talked about cash flow. Cash flow is made up of two things:

1. Money in (income)
2. Money out (expenses)

What Future You needs to know is that, to get wealthy, you need to pull your head out of your cash flow and start thinking about your **balance sheet.**

Your balance sheet is also made up of two things:

1. Assets (things you have)
2. Debts (things you owe)

The difference between what you have and what you owe is called your **net worth**. Wealthy people have a high net worth. I know there are a lot of new words here, but they're important words, I promise!

How you start to get wealthy, and build your freedom, is by spending less than you earn and by taking the difference and saving it.

When you've saved money, you can use it to reduce a debt, or you can buy assets with it.

Now, not everything you own is an **asset**. Assets are things you own that will **increase in value over time**, or **things that will earn you money**. A new Nintendo isn't an asset, because if you try to sell it in a few years' time it will be worth less than what you paid for it. Some things – like really old cars, for example – are worth MORE the longer you own them. If you're a photographer, owning a camera can be an asset, because you can use it to earn money.

Now, let's say that you put your snorgles on a diet, so they eat fewer apples. You now have more apples than your snorgles can eat, so you save some of your apples, and plant the seeds so that they turn into apple trees – those apple trees are an asset, and the act of planting the seeds is called **investing**.

SAVINGS   INCOME   EXPENSES

Soon your apple trees start producing their own apples. YAY, APPLES FOR DAYS! You can use these apples to plant even more apple trees. Eventually, you can adopt even more snorgles, and still have enough to save.

At some point, your apple trees are growing all the apples you'll ever need, so you can quit your apple-picking job and spend all your time teaching your snorgles to hula hoop.

In this example, someone has bought a lot of **assets**, which means they're earning **passive income**.

ASSET

INCOME FROM YOUR JOB

INCOME FROM YOUR ASSETS   EXPENSES

In fact, it turns out that the amount you save is the single most important part of being a grownup with your money.

Once your money's on your balance sheet, figuring out how to make it grow and turn it into **passive income** actually isn't all that difficult.

There are two ways in which you keep more money. You can either earn more, or you can spend your money more smartly than everyone else does. But it doesn't matter how much you earn, unless you're keeping a lot of it and building up a bunch of assets. That's how we get ahead.

Assets don't have to be boring, either! This book you're holding is one of my **assets**: I wrote a book (and it was really fun for me to write), and that book will now go out into the world, earning money for me for a long time afterwards.[19] Assets can be things you really care about: art you make or a business you own.

WHO WANTS TO BE A MILLIONAIRE?

> It's not how much you make, it's how much you keep.
> – *The Bogleheads' Guide to Investing*

So, who wants to be a millionaire? Maybe a better question is, what kind of salary will let you become a millionaire? R50k a month? R100k a month?

Let's say that you start earning a salary of R10 000 a month when you're 25 (that's about what a new primary-school teacher at a government school earns). And that you work for 40 years until you retire at 65. Let's imagine that nothing ever goes wrong and you never miss a paycheque in all that time, but you also never get a promotion and improve your

---

19 Digby says thanks for the cat food.

salary – you just earn R10 000 every month for 40 years. That would mean that you, with a very ordinary R10 000 salary, would earn nearly R5 million in your lifetime. Five million smackaroos would buy you something like 160 000 Big Macs and a lot of heartburn.

How many years it will take you to earn your first million rand
(assuming your salary remains the same)

Monthly salary	Years to earn a million
R5 000	17
R10 000	8
R15 000	6
R20 000	4
R25 000	3

In fact, it turns out that MOST people earn many millions of rands over their lifetimes. You probably will too! So, why aren't most people millionaires?

Simple: because they spend nearly all of their money.

If you were earning your R10 000 a month from age 25, and saved **a third** of it every month in a shoebox, you'd have saved a million bucks by age 41.

How much you would have saved by age 65					
Monthly salary	Total earned	Save 5%	Save 10%	Save 20%	Save 30%
10 000	19 805 722	990 286	1 980 572	3 961 144	5 941 717
15 000	29 708 583	1 485 429	2 970 858	5 941 717	8 912 575
20 000	39 611 444	1 980 572	3 961 144	7 922 289	11 883 433
25 000	49 514 305	2 475 715	4 951 431	9 902 861	14 854 292
30 000	59 417 166	2 970 858	5 941 717	11 883 433	17 825 150
35 000	69 320 027	3 466 001	6 932 003	13 864 005	20 796 008
40 000	79 222 888	3 961 144	7 922 289	15 844 578	23 766 866

Now pretend you have a cousin, Bigshot. Bigshot starts his first job at age 25 earning a smooth R30k a month, three times as much as you and your puny R10k, but he only saves 5% of it. It's going to take Bigshot until he's 55 years old to save his first million, even though Bigshot will earn nearly R60 million over his lifetime. Now, Bigshot might have had a great time spending all that extra money. He might even look like a **rich** person. But you, with your savings, are going to become **wealthy** much more quickly than he is.

Here's how I think about the difference between rich people and wealthy people:

Rich people have *spent* a lot of money. They own a lot of nice things: they have the swanky clothes and the big car and the nice house. But they might have used debt to buy all their nice things, which means they don't *really* own them. Rich people are often very stressed out because of their debt, and they usually don't have a lot of freedom because they're worried about how to pay for the stuff they've bought. Rich people often have a LOT of snorgles, and are also looking after some HUGE Interest Monsters, so they have to spend all their time picking apples.

The worst part is, a lot of people have been duped into thinking that their *expenses* are *assets*. It's not rich people's fault that this happens: people in the advertising industry make it their whole job to convince people that things like expensive cars are assets (but most cars aren't – they're expenses).

Wealthy people have *saved* a lot of money. They might have chosen NOT to buy all the fancy things for themselves, because they've rather bought assets (rather than adopting extra snorgles, they've planted a lot of apple trees). So, the funny thing about wealthy people is that sometimes they look poor, because they don't own fancy things! But you can't

A STRESSED RICH PERSON:

YOUR HOUSE

INTEREST ON YOUR HOUSE

INCOME FROM YOUR JOB

EXPENSES

I.O.U

LIABILITIES

really tell if a person is wealthy from looking at the stuff they own – you'd have to peek at their bank account.

A WEALTHY PERSON:

But here's the thing: because of **compound interest**, money that you save grows in time, and it grows and grows and grows. Sacrificing nice things when you're young means that you get LOTS more of the good things when you're older. Wealthy people usually end up with more money than they can even spend, eventually. But it takes a lot of time and patience.

So, this is the big thing that you really, really need to understand.

Earning all the money in the world will not make you wealthy, unless you save some of that money. And the opposite is true: you can earn your freedom by having the discipline to save more of your salary, even if it's pretty small. Compound interest can only do its magic on money that you've **saved**.

So, when you're young, **learning how to save is like getting your Hogwarts letter**: it's proof that you're a wizard or witch, and you can make magic with your money.

Ask your favourite adult if they'll do a compound interest challenge with you! Here's what you'll need:
1. A glass jar
2. A box of your favourite small treats (like Smarties or nuts, or you can do this with real cash if your adult is keen)
3. A permanent marker (optional)

This might look like a game for kiddies, but it's also a great way to dupe your folks into buying you snacks ;) Here's how the challenge works:
1. Start off by putting one of the treats in the jar. The adult keeps the rest of them (they have to promise not to steal any). The jar is the 'bank account', and the adult is the 'bank'. Count the treats in the box so you know how many there are.
2. The adult gets to set a **compound interest rate** for the jar. They might choose to set 5%, 10%, 50% or 100%, depending on how old you are and how many treats you've got.

3. Every morning, the adult will pay you 'interest' into the jar in the form of more treats, until all the treats are in the jar. Say you're working on a 50% interest rate and there are three treats in the jar; the adult will add 1½ new treats to the jar on that day.

4. On day 1, you guess how many days it will take before all of the treats have moved from the box into the jar. Write that number on the jar with a permanent marker, so you don't forget.

5. If you guess right, you get to eat all the treats! If you guess wrong, the adult gets to eat HALF of them (you still get to eat the other half because you're awesome and I like you and I make the rules).

IN SUMMARY!

- Compound interest makes money HULK OUT.
- The single most important factor in growing your money with compound interest is time. The longer you leave your money to compound, the bigger it will get. That's why starting young is so important.
- Compound interest applies to debt, too, so the longer you take to pay back money you owe, the more money you'll pay.

Chapter 4

THE WORLD AROUND YOU

LIFE IS HARDER FOR SOME PEOPLE THAN IT IS FOR OTHERS

I want you to imagine two identical twin babies, Blue and Jade. Blue and Jade have exactly the same DNA: they are born with exactly the same talents and potential. But they're going to have very different lives.

Imagine that Blue and Jade's parents die in an accident just after they're born[20] and they're adopted into different families. Both of their new families love the babies very much, but there's one big difference: Blue's new family is wealthy, and Jade's new family is poor.

Let's think about how Blue's life and Jade's life might be different.

Blue	Jade
As a baby Blue gets fed well. She grows up strong and healthy, and has lots of energy to learn and play.	**As a baby** Jade sometimes doesn't get all of the nutrients she needs to grow. She is sometimes hungry and has less energy.

---

20 If it helps, imagine it was a non-tragic accident like getting licked to death by puppies.

When she starts school Blue struggles to learn how to read, but her teacher realises that she has bad eyesight. Her parents buy glasses for her, and soon Blue learns to read and write. Her home is filled with books, so she grows up with a love of reading.

Primary school is really fun for Blue! She is in a small class so she gets lots of attention from her teachers. After school, she has playdates at her friends' houses or gets taken on adventures by her au pair. She only has a few chores, because her family can afford a domestic worker.

In high school Blue starts to struggle with maths, so her parents get her a private tutor to help her. She finishes matric with great marks and is awarded a scholarship for a university.

When she starts school Jade struggles to learn to read, but because there are so many kids in her class no one ever notices that her eyesight is the problem. Jade gets frustrated with books and doesn't understand why reading is so much harder for her than for her friends.

Primary school is tough for Jade. She has teachers who care a lot, but her teachers run much bigger classes and are always tired and grumpy. After school, she has to do a lot of chores at home and doesn't have much time to play or do extramurals.

In high school Jade starts to struggle with maths. There's no one to help her. She does her best, though, and manages to pass matric, but doesn't get university entrance.

After school Blue decides she wants to help sick people. She goes to university and gets a degree in physiotherapy. Her parents buy her a car and pay for her living costs, so she graduates without any debt.

After school Jade decides she wants to help sick people. She takes out a loan to get a nursing diploma from a TVET college. She has to work side-jobs to support herself while she's studying, so she's always tired.

When she starts working Blue is excited to get her first paycheque – it's R30 000 a month! She still has the car her parents bought her, and she doesn't have big expenses, so she has plenty of money to start saving and buying assets.

When she starts working Jade is excited to get her first paycheque – it's R16 000 a month! But a big chunk of every paycheque goes to paying off her student loans. She also sends money home to help out her little brother and her parents. This leaves her with barely enough to get by, so she's got nothing left to save.

It's not impossible for Jade to end up having a richer, happier, easier, luckier life than Blue. But Jade's had a much harder start. Jade will have to work harder than Blue to catch up, even though she has exactly the same abilities as Blue does. That seems horribly unfair, doesn't it?

We could say that Blue is more **privileged** than Jade, because she had a whole bunch of things that made it easier for her to succeed. Things like tutors, a good school, better healthcare, all the things that wealth can buy in a country like South Africa . . . these are like power-ups in a video game. They make it easier for you to win.

Being privileged doesn't make Blue a bad person. It doesn't mean that she should be punished for her success, or that she didn't work hard for it. It just means she was lucky.

It's up to your generation to decide what type of world you're going to build when you're older. I hope you decide to build one where there are fewer ways for people to be unlucky, and where children have equal opportunities no matter what kind of families they're born into.

What are some of your privileges? Here are some ideas to get you started:

Being healthy

Living without disabilities

Having adults in your life who care about you

A good school

Not having died by excessive puppy-licking ...

Having access to books.

MONEY ISN'T A BOYS' GAME

Let's talk for a minute about why learning how money works is especially important for a woman.

On average, South African women earn nearly 30% less than South African men. This gender pay gap is a global problem, and it happens for many reasons.

1. Women are encouraged from a young age to build different kinds of skills that lead them into different kinds

of jobs, and those jobs are less well paid. We buy little girls dolls and little boys Lego, and then we pay engineers more than we pay child-carers.

2. Women are paid less for doing the same jobs that men do. This can be because people who set women's salaries unconsciously assume they're less good at their jobs than they are. It doesn't help that girls are taught from a young age to be nice rather than firm, which means women are less likely to insist that they get paid what they deserve.

3. Women are still responsible for the lion's share of family care and housework (not to mention that some of them take several months off work to create HUMAN LIFE because they're magical like that). This all accounts for years of unpaid work that women do over their lifetimes, and it takes a lot of time out of their careers.

So, women earn less. That's bad enough. Then, to make matters worse, women have higher lifetime expenses than men do:

1. Generally, women live longer than men do (by a full seven years!), which means women spend much more money on retirement and old-age healthcare expenses.

2. In our country, almost half of all mothers are single, and only 15% of fathers in divorced households contribute financially. Kids ain't cheap.

3. The beauty and fashion industries have been built around making women feel like they need to spend a preposterous amount of money every year just to look acceptable to the world. The stress and expense of this can be even worse if you're trans, queer or non-binary.

There are a hundred other reasons I could list, but I get so angry thinking about this that I need to stop now.

Fellow girls, hear me for a moment. You are probably going to live longer. You are probably going to earn less than you should earn. It's unfair, and we must fight it.

Girls should care even more about learning how money works than boys do. Yet, weirdly, people are going to assume that money's not something you want to worry your pretty little head about. They'll make jokes about how your money plan should just be to find yourself a nice husband.

And even worse? Part of you may believe them. You'll have moments of second-guessing yourself and wondering whether you will ever understand any of this money stuff.

Don't let this happen to you. You can't single-handedly remove gender bias from the world. But you can fight it in your own mind. You can refuse to accept the story that you're 'just a girl' and should leave all this money stuff to the big boys.

SOUTH AFRICA IS AN UNFAIR PLACE

South Africa is actually one of the most unequal countries in the world. This didn't happen by accident. Our nation was founded on a system called colonialism, where foreign countries took control of this land and tried to steal all the valuable stuff from it, stuff like gold and coal. All around the world, to support this aim, human beings were transported across the world and forced into slavery. Entire cultures were destroyed. For hundreds of years, South Africa was governed by these colonial governments, whether Dutch or British.

And when the Nationalist Party won the 1948 election and implemented their policy of apartheid, they created laws to take further wealth from black people and give it to white people. You see, every day, the toll this has had on human lives. The stories of our bloody, evil past are still written all over our country.

And it's not like the impact of this all just evaporated overnight in 1994 when Madiba made rainbow clouds spout from his feet and everything was suddenly right again. We're still recovering from our history.

Here are some facts for you: there are 59 million people in South Africa. Half of those people are classified as poor. The majority of poor people are black. About 40% of black South Africans are unemployed, as opposed to 8% of white people. The average income of white South African households is more than five times the average for black households. And 70% of the top management of South African businesses[21] are . . . you guessed it . . . white people. And mostly dudes.[22]

It's not that all white people in South Africa are richer than all black people; but it's true that white people are, on average, *much luckier*. That's what is meant by the term 'white privilege'.

South Africa's economy has other problems, too. Wealth in our country isn't spread out very well. Too much of the wealth and power is tied up in only a few businesses, and also in the government (with not enough checks and balances). Research shows that the share of South Africa's wealth owned

---

21 (The ones that have more than 50 employees or are big enough to have to report this.)

22 Source: https://africacheck.org/reports/race-poverty-and-inequality-black-first-land-first-claims-fact-checked/

by the top 1% of earners has doubled since the late 1970s.[23] So, inequality isn't even getting better – it's getting worse. It's getting even harder for people like Jade to succeed.

> Guess how rich your family is compared to the average South African household income. Then ask your folks to show you the real answer on this website: https://www.saldru.uct.ac.za/income-comparison-tool/

SOME COUNTRIES ARE RICHER THAN OTHERS

There is inequality within countries, but there's also a lot of inequality *between* countries. Some countries are richer than others. For example, the average Australian's net worth is about R2.9 million, compared to the average South African's net worth, which is R39 000.

This is partly because different countries have different economies. In some countries, most of the wealth is created from selling off natural resources like oil and gold (this tends to make for unequal and corrupt economies). In other countries, more of the wealth is created from making stuff in factories or growing food, and in others, it's from stuff like running banks or building websites or making movies. Countries trade stuff with each other all the time: the iPad you've been putting on your birthday wish list is built in China, using a lot of materials that come from Africa, and it was designed in America. If country A buys more stuff from country B than they sell to country B, then country A will

---

23 Source: World Wealth and Income Database, Thomas Piketty and Emmanuel Saez.

gradually get poorer than country B (the fancy name for this is a 'trade deficit').

Most countries have their own currency, the type of money that they use to buy stuff. Currencies do not have the same values. One rand is not worth the same as one US dollar or one Kenyan shilling. Here are some rough examples.[24]

Country	Currency	Value
South Africa	Rand (ZAR)	–
United States	Dollar (USD)	1 USD = 15 ZAR
Nigeria	Naira (NGN)	1 NGN = 0.04 ZAR
China	Yuan/Renminbi (CNY)	1 CNY = 2 ZAR
Mexico	Peso (MXN)	1 MXN = 0.8 ZAR
Kenya	Shilling (KES)	1 KES = 0.15 ZAR

Let's say you go visit your mom's sister in the US. You can't spend rands while you're there, so when you get off the plane in New York you need to swap your rands for dollars. You used to have to actually go to a special kind of shop that would do that for you (called a Bureau de Change), but now banks all run on computers so you can do it through an app, or by just spending on a bank card like normal. When you swap your rands for dollars, the 'price' that you get for your rands is called the exchange rate.

These rates change all the time, which affects how much your money is worth in another country. If the exchange rate improves in your favour, your rand is worth more (it's a strong

24   This stuff goes out of date VERY quickly. These numbers are accurate as I'm writing this book in February 2020, but it will probably already have changed a lot by the time you're reading it. Also, hello from the past! What's it like to live in the future?

rand). But if the rates go against you, your rand can be worth less (a weak rand). One day, an iPad costing $400 can cost you R5 790. A few hours later, even though it still costs $400, it could actually cost you R6 200, because of the exchange rate changing.

Exchange rates change for many reasons, and one of these is how much growth there is in the economy, which affects how much money people from other countries are prepared to put into businesses in the country. Political instability will make a difference, and so will how people in other countries view a country's political leadership.

Generally, a strong currency *tends* to be a sign that your economy is doing well, but that's not always true. Japan has one of the strongest economies in the world, but the value of a Japanese yen is very low. Exchange rates are complicated, yo.

Although some of the world's inequality is because of how economies are today, a lot of it is also because of how economies were in the past. A lot of this goes back to colonialism, and how money was made in some parts of the world (like Europe) at the expense of other parts, including Africa. Colonialism happened over 200 years ago, so just imagine what compounding has done to that wealth by now!

WHAT'S BONKERS ABOUT BILLIONAIRES

It's when you put those two types of inequality together – inequality *between* countries, and inequality *within* countries – that things start to get really nuts. The really richest people in the world, the billionaires, have so much money that it's hard to even imagine what having that much money means.

In Chapter 3, we spoke about how all of us are actually likely to earn many millions of rands in our lifetimes. So the idea that you, the very charming young person holding this book right now, might become a millionaire one day is actually very possible (I'd even say, likely!). And being a billionaire sounds just a bit better than being a millionaire, right?

- A million is a thousand thousand. It has six zeros:
  1 000 000
- A billion is a thousand million. It has nine zeros:
  1 000 000 000
- A trillion is a thousand billion. It has 12 zeros:
  1 000 000 000 000

The problem is, our puny human brains can't actually understand how big those numbers are. Once we get beyond what we can count on our fingers and toes, a big number doesn't feel that much bigger than another big number. But a million is actually VERY different from a billion. And a trillion is just . . . like . . . insane. Like your brain would explode if it were to really grasp how big a trillion is.

Here's a different way to understand how different those numbers are:

- A million seconds is 12 days.
- A billion seconds is 32 years!
- Okay, okay, but a trillion seconds is 30 000 years!!!
  30 000 years ago cavemen were just discovering this radical new technology called MAKING TOOLS OUT OF STONE.

Or, here's another way to see it.

- If we divided up R1 million among all 56 million South Africans, we'd each get 2 cents *crickets*.
- If we divided up R1 billion, we'd each get a little under R20. Nice! We could each buy a coke and a bag of chips.

* If we divided up R1 trillion, we'd each get R20 000 and everyone could buy FOUR NEW XBOXES.[25]

Or, if you want to see it visually:

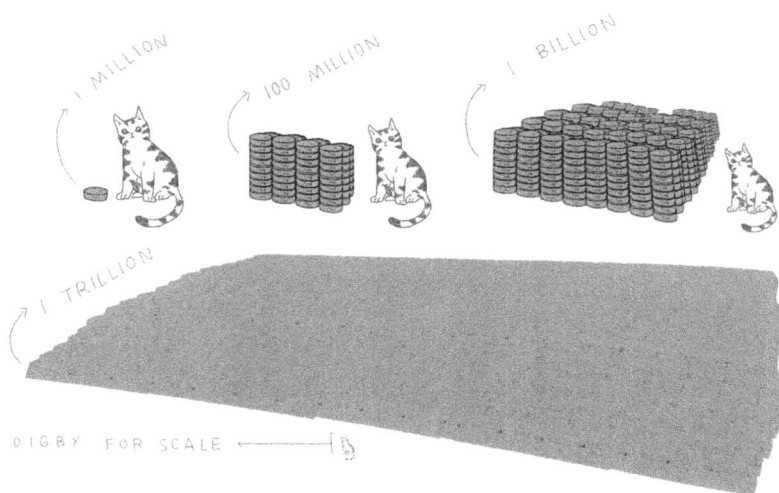

The richest person in the world today is Jeff Bezos, the guy who started Amazon. Jeff Bezos has a net worth of $126 billion, which is nearly R2 trillion. Jeff Bezos could personally end world hunger, he could build every homeless person in the world a small house, he could buy a mansion in every country on earth that's so big that it has a private bowling alley and a cinema.[26] Jeff Bezos spending R600 million is the same as the average South African spending R1.

25 Thanks to this News24 article for that example: https://www.news24. com/MyNews24/How-much-is-a-billion-rand-20141002

26 Here are a bunch of other nuts things that Jeff Bezos could do with his money: https://www.boredpanda.com/rich-billionaire-money-worth-explained-thelastmemeera/

It's not just Jeff Bezos, though. The richest 85 people in the world today are worth more than the poorest HALF of the world's people. And the world is becoming a more unequal place every day, meaning that it is becoming harder and harder for people who are born poor to become rich over their lifetimes. What's the best way to become rich? Be born rich. In other words, inheriting wealth gives you a huge advantage over others.

My point is, if you feel like the system is rigged against you because you weren't born rich, that's because it is. Doubly so if you're a woman. Quadruply so if you're black. (Take note of this if you were born rich, male or white.)

And while this book is going to help you to use money better, both now and in the future, it doesn't mean that, if you get it right, it's because you're a better person than other people. Do not blame the poor for their poverty. The poor are not poor because they're not working hard enough, or because they're stupid, or because they're not managing their money well. They're poor because the system is broken, and rigged against everyone except for a tiny group of people at the top. And it's rigged much more against some people than against others.

While we do what we can to have a healthy relationship with this green magic money juice, it must not stop us from finding out about, and trying to fix, the system that has made us so vulnerable to begin with, and has shut so many people out completely.

The world doesn't have to be so unfair. There are things we can do to make it fairer. We'll talk more about that in Chapter 11.

IN SUMMARY!

- The world today is very unfair. We don't all start out with the same opportunities, and some people have to work harder than others to succeed. And some people just have WAY too much money (billionaires).
- South Africa is one of the most unequal countries in the world.
- We can all improve our chances of succeeding by understanding money better, but that doesn't mean that people who are poor have done something wrong.
- The world doesn't have to be as unfair as it is. It's your generation's responsibility to make it fairer.[27]

---

27 Sorry about that. My generation was busy trying to convince Boomers that climate change exists, and also mucking about on Tumblr.

PART 2

MAKING

MONEY

Chapter 5
ALLOWANCES

This theory stuff is fine and all, but you'll only really learn the rules of money when you're managing some of it for real. It's like thinking that reading a book about singing will teach you to sing well. SPOILER ALERT: it won't (I have read a lot of books about famous singers, and my singing sounds like a cat that's choking on gravel).

So let's talk about some ways we can start putting real cash in your pocket, right now. You can tell your folks it's for 'learning purposes' if you like, but let's be honest: I also want you to have money so you can start saving up for some of the kiff[28] stuff you want.

There are three main ways you could be earning money as a kid:

1. **Pocket money or an allowance.** An allowance is a set, regular amount you are given from a guardian or parent. Pocket money is money you're just given as and when, like if your folks give you money if you're going out to a movie.

2. **Money you earn**, perhaps through working at certain chores, or by selling stuff you've made, or even by taking part in the odd highly paid job (like being a model at a

---

28 I'm really old, okay? I still use the word 'kiff' unironically. One day you'll be old and kids will laugh at you for still saying 'dank' or whatever.

photoshoot, or working as Batman's sidekick over your summer holidays). We'll call these your side-hustles. Why? Because, at this point in your life, your main hustle is being at school!

3. **Gifts.** In some families and cultures, kids get money for big milestones (like a bat or bar mitzvah, a 13th birthday or sweet 16th) or holidays (birthdays, Eid or Christmas).

You can't really control what gifts you get, so we'll focus on the other two.

Lucky money

Some kids have other types of money in their life, like money that's been invested on their behalf, or money that they inherited or got from life insurance because someone they love died, or a pile of gold doubloons buried in their garden because their parents are pirates. Sometimes, money like this is controlled by a **trust**, which is like a business that looks after a family's money for them. We're not going to be talking about that kind of money here, because it's very rare, you don't have control over whether you get it or not, and it's not money that you're actively managing.

PRACTISE MAKES PERFECT

Have you ever watched nature videos about baby birds learning to fly? When the baby bird is very small, it never leaves the nest, and the mother bird will bring back delicious worm goop[29] and drop it straight into the baby's mouth. When

---

29 Delicious for baby birds, that is. I don't recommend you try eating worm goop.

the baby gets a bit bigger, the mother bird will start holding the food out a little way away from the nest, so the baby has to learn how to use its legs to come get it. The mother bird teaches the baby to stretch its wings, and then how to flap them. It's a slow, gradual process: the baby birds learn how to survive by themselves bit by bit.

Now, imagine what it would be like if, instead, the mother bird just fed the bird in the nest every day until the bird was grown, and then one day just yeeted the baby bird out into the sky and hoped for the best? It would be brutal!

Allowances are a great way for you to practise managing your own money, so that one day when you move out of home you don't feel like you've just been yeeted into the sky before you've been taught how to fly. When I moved out of home, I was a fool and accidentally spent all my grocery money on Lego in the first two weeks, and then didn't have money for food. DON'T BE LIKE ME. Practise being responsible with your money!

I'm going to say it again – families are different, and what I'm going to suggest here doesn't work for every family.

The case for getting an allowance

There are a lot of really good reasons for kids to get an allowance.

- Research shows that kids who get an allowance show better self-control when it comes to spending, because they've had more practise at managing their own money.[30] We'll be talking about how to actually manage your money in Chapter 8.

---

30 This is from research done by Rona Abramovitch, Jonathan L. Freedman and Patricia Pliner.

- It's a great way for you to learn how to save up for things you really want.
- Your folks are already spending money on you. An allowance isn't necessarily costing your folks more money, it's just about YOU having more control over what that money's spent on.
- If you get an allowance, you can spend less time looking for side-hustles, so you can focus on school.

The case against getting an allowance

There are good reasons why your folks might not want to give you an allowance. That's fine, too! We'll talk about what to do if they're dead set against it a bit later.

- Your folks might believe it's better for you to earn your own money, because that's an important life lesson (when you're an adult, no one's going to give you an allowance – you'll have to work for money).[31]
- Your family might not be able to afford it.
- Some families believe that children having their own money encourages selfishness – they prefer for everyone to think of the family's money as belonging to everyone in the family.
- You might have older siblings who didn't get an allowance, so your getting one might not feel fair.
- Your folks might not trust you to make good decisions with your money, or feel like if you have extra money you'll spend it on stuff that isn't good for you, like sweets or attack spiders.

---

31 Unless you're the Queen of England – she sorta gets an allowance (and hello, Your Majesty! I'm so pleased you're reading this book!). Or one day in the future the world might decide that everyone should get a universal basic income, which is kind of like an allowance for adults. That would be pretty awesome.

● It might not have been a normal part of your folks' money culture growing up, so it might just seem like a weird idea to them that they don't understand.

DIFFERENT TYPES OF ALLOWANCES

An allowance can work in different ways. Some options are:

1. A **regular allowance** that you get once a week or once a month. It's always the same amount, and you get it no matter what.
2. A **conditional allowance** where you get paid for doing chores around the house, or for keeping your marks high at school.
3. A **mixed allowance** where you get a regular allowance but can also earn extra cash for doing *special* chores.

Personally, I'm a fan of a **mixed allowance**. Getting a regular amount once a month is a good way for you to start learning how to manage money, because you'll need to learn how to pace yourself and not spend EVERYTHING on the first day by buying up every single thing at the tuck shop. But – if your folks can afford it – it's also nice to be able to earn extra amounts for doing especially big or gross jobs around the house, like cleaning out that one Tupperware that's been in the fridge for so long it's growing a whole botanical garden inside.

I'm generally on your side about everything, I promise, but I don't think that you should get paid for doing *normal* chores around the house (stuff like folding your clothes or helping clear the table or doing dishes). Doing chores is just part of life, and it's part of being a good family member to help each other and make sure that one person (often a woman) isn't having to do all the work for everyone else. I also don't personally like the idea of getting paid to do well at school, because you should have different motivations for school beyond money. The chores you might want to ask to get paid to do are things that your folks are currently doing themselves, or paying someone else to do, like maybe cleaning the pool or organising the cupboards.

I also think that, if you get an allowance, it should increase every year, but that the things that your allowance needs to cover should increase too. When you're younger, it's fine for an allowance to be just for luxuries like special treats or games. If you run out of money before the next allowance payment, it's no biggie – you might just have to wait a few extra weeks before you can buy that new skin for your avatar. But when you get older, it's good practise also to be managing the money for your clothes, extramurals and toiletries. Remember, you don't want to be yeeted into the sky like a baby bird the day school ends.

HOW TO ASK FOR AN ALLOWANCE (OR FOR A BIGGER ALLOWANCE)

The most important rule is to **do your homework** before you ask your folks about something big like an allowance. Before you have the conversation, you should practise your reasons for wanting an allowance, and be specific about what you propose the allowance covers. You should also think about alternatives to an allowance, in case your folks say no.

Choose the right time to have the conversation. Don't ask them when they're stressed or in a hurry or busy doing something else. This is also definitely a conversation to have IRL, not over text.

It's a good idea to set up a specific time to have the conversation. For instance, you might go to them in the morning and say something like, '[Mum/Dad/Ouma/Batman], can we have a chat tonight after supper, please? I want to talk to you about getting an allowance.' It's better if they don't feel like you've sprung this on them out of nowhere.

When it comes to the chat itself, here's an example of what types of things you might say:

> Oh glorious wonderful [parent-type person]! (*A little bit of flattery never hurts.*)
>
> You know that great book about money I've been reading? It's made me think that I want to start practising managing my own money. I think a good way for me to do that will be to get a monthly allowance.
>
> *Explain some of the other reasons that you want to get an allowance, like maybe it will mean that you don't have to look for side-hustles so you can focus on school.*
>
> *Then explain what you'd want to do with that allowance. It could be stuff like this:*
>
> I also want to practise saving up for my goals, because this is an important skill to learn! I've been thinking that I want to open a savings account and save up for [a new game console/light-up sneakers/whatever].
>
> I also plan to give 10% of my allowance to charity.
>
> I want to practise budgeting, so I want to start buying my own toiletries/clothes out of my allowance.

Then, ask them for their thoughts. It's important to LISTEN to them. If they say they have reservations, ask questions so you can understand their point of view. You don't need to win the negotiation today: play the long game. Your main goal for the first chat is to get information, so that you can go off and think about the questions your folks might have, and think about good answers to them. You will probably need to have two or three conversations about this before they agree.

It's good to talk about a lot of different alternatives, so it's not a simple 'yes' or 'no' question. Discuss conditional allowances versus fixed or mixed allowances. Ask if there are any big chores they'd consider paying you to do. Ask if they'd consider letting you manage money they're already spending on you, rather than just giving you fun money. In any negotiation, you want to find solutions that feel like BOTH of you are winning, and getting something you want. So figure out something they want! Maybe they'll agree to it if you keep a budget, so you can show them you're practising a skill.

If all else fails, you could always DISTRACT THEM BY WEARING A FAKE HEAD SO THEY GET CONFUSED AND THINK THERE ARE TWO OF YOU. Just kidding.

These things are NOT a good argument:

- 'But everyone else in my school gets one!'
- 'I have the right to an allowance!'
- 'You *have* to give me an allowance!'

If you have a few chats with your folks, and their answer is no, you need to accept that. Most kids in the world don't get an allowance, and there's no charter of Kids' Rights that says everyone is entitled to one. I'm certain that your folks are already working hard to make sure that your family has what it needs, and an allowance just might not be in the family's budget right now. Respect that.

WHAT IF YOU CAN'T GET AN ALLOWANCE?

Never fear! You can still find other ways to get some spare dough in your pocket.

- Ask if you can help to manage the family expenses, so that you can still practise having to work to a budget. For example, if you have a pet, can you be in charge of buying food for the pet? Can you try to figure out how to stretch the weekly grocery money one week? If your family is big on buying gifts, could you be the one who's in charge of the gifts budget for a while?
- Find a side-hustle! We'll talk more about this in a bit.
- Ask your folks, neighbours or extended family if there are any special jobs they'd be willing to pay you to do.
- Ask your folks if they'd be able to match your savings towards a goal. Say, for every R10 that you earn from a side-hustle, they'll put in an extra R10.

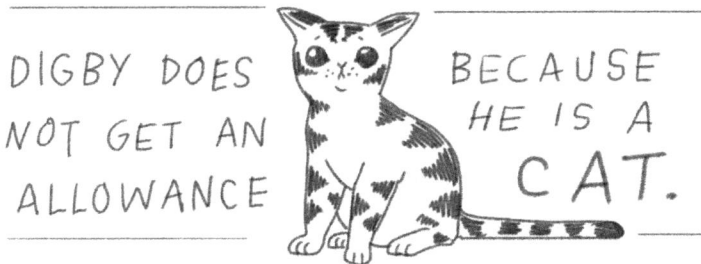

DIGBY DOES NOT GET AN ALLOWANCE BECAUSE HE IS A CAT.

Here are some ideas for bigger chores that your family or neighbours might be willing to pay you to do:

- Wash windows inside and out
- Clear out that one room/shed/garage that's piled up with boxes no one ever uses[32]

---

32 . . . and spiders. So many spiders . . .

- Vacuum and shampoo the couches
- Wash the car
- Do stuff in the garden, like mowing a lawn, weeding or planting trees
- Polish shoes
- Wash out the inside of the dustbins
- Mend clothes (this is also a great skill to have for after the zombie apocalypse)

SOME THINGS TO THINK ABOUT

Do you know how much pocket money your friends get? Do you think it's helpful to know what your friends get? Why, or why not?

IN SUMMARY!

- It's important to find a way to have some money to manage now, so that you can practise skills you'll need later in your life.
- There are strong arguments for and against getting an allowance. In the end, it's a conversation you'll have to have with your folks.
- When you have the chat with your folks about getting an allowance, go in with an open mind and listen to their concerns.

Chapter 6

THE ART OF THE SIDE-HUSTLE

SIDE-HUSTLES RULE

I'm a firm believer that everyone needs a side-hustle, no matter how busy you are with school, sport and snoozing.[33] Why?

- You'll learn awesome new skills.
- In this world, you can't always rely on someone else giving you a job. A lot of people in the world are unemployed. It's important to learn how to make your own jobs.
- You'll learn how to manage a business, and how to motivate yourself.
- You'll learn more about yourself and what you actually love (you won't ever discover your secret deep love of baking cabbage cookies until you try!).
- It's the best way to make an extra few hundred bucks, right now.

Having a side-hustle basically means being an entrepreneur. An entrepreneur is someone who makes money by running their own business. These businesses can sell goods or they

---

33 I'm a big believer in naps. Taking a 20-minute nap every afternoon after coming home from school is the only thing that saved me from crashing and burning out in high school, and since then I've arranged my entire career around being able to take a nap every day. You're allowed to take a lot of naps when you're a writer.

can sell services. The best thing about being an entrepreneur is that you are 100% the boss and no one can tell you what to do.

Becoming an entrepreneur teaches you a useful set of skills, no matter what you end up doing with your life later. Entrepreneurs aren't just people who run shops or invent things: artists, musicians, actors, Instagram celebrities, sports stars . . . they're all entrepreneurs.

The thing about being an entrepreneur is that **most businesses you start will fail**, so you've got to start a lot of businesses. It's like those really hard video games where you just have to play the same level over and over again until you get it. Being really smart or really talented won't help you; you will probably still have to fail a bunch of times before something you try works. That's why being a kid entrepreneur is so great: failing doesn't matter so much. That means you've got lots of time to try things and learn a bunch of important lessons about running your own business at a time in your life when it's safe to do this (no one's going to kick you out of your home if your business fails – you're just a kid!).

One of the most important things you might learn in your whole life is that failing is okay. Failing is how you learn. Do not be scared to do new things and fail. Learning to carry on after failing is tough. But if you can do it, you're going to go far.[34]

---

34 This is a lesson that it took me a LONG time to learn. When I was a kid, I was so scared of failing that I only ever did stuff I knew I was already good at (in other words, I managed to make excuses to get out of ever playing any sports because I was as graceful as a boneless giraffe on ice skates). Eventually, I realised that only doing stuff you're already good at makes you a very boring person who never learns anything new, and means you'll miss out on a lot of experiences that might make you really happy.

LET'S BRAINSTORM SIDE-HUSTLE IDEAS!

Finding the perfect side-hustle is about matching up two things:

1. What you can become good at (your *skills*). It's fine if you're not good at it now, but you must be willing to practise it enough to become good at it. That means you should find it at least a little bit interesting.
2. What people want (what's *valued*). Other people must feel that what you are selling is valuable enough for them to pay for.

STEP 1: Skills and interests

Let's start with your *skills* and *interests*. Go through this list and circle the things that you've got the skills to do, or that you're interested in and would like to learn about.

Services

- Any of the special home chores we discussed in the previous chapter, like washing cars – could you do them for neighbours?
- Do a basic bike service or fix punctures
- Tech support, like helping an old fogey set up their phone or upgrade their computer
- Ironing
- Perform at younger kids' parties – for instance, could you learn how to do magic tricks or play an instrument?
- Look after pets or walk dogs
- Build basic websites (you could use an online service like Wix, Squarespace or WordPress)

- Photography or video editing
- Digitise people's photos using something like the Photo-Scan app
- Tutoring on school subjects you're good at (you could even do this online)
- Graphic design – making posters, social media posts and logos (apps like Over and Canva make this easy)
- Book-covering/name-tape sewing service for parents of younger kids at back-to-school time

Can you think of any other useful skills you have, or that you'd like to have?

If you don't know how to do these things, they're all easy to learn through online courses. There's a list of great, kid-friendly online courses on the website.

Goods (things you could sell)
- Knitted beanies or scarves
- Worm tea[35]
- Baked goods
- Buying sweets/cold drinks/stickers/whatever at a low price and selling them at a higher price (the trick to this is finding a place to buy them that's really cheap, like a mega discount store, or buying them online)
- Custom T-shirts/hats/hoodies/stickers (maybe featuring memes that are big at your school right now, or school team logos)
- Seedlings of indigenous plants
- Custom-painted sneakers

---

35 Not as gross as it sounds. Google it :)

- You could look at buying something expensive that people only use sometimes, and renting it out – for instance, a marquee tent people use for weddings, or power tools
- Ask if you can sell things your family isn't using any more on Gumtree or Facebook (please do ASK them first, don't just start selling off your sister's takkies!)
- Upcycled crafts made out of recycled materials, like rugs made out of plastic bags

Can you think of anything else you could sell?

You'll probably have to try a few different side-hustles before you find one that works. Be valiant, brave entrepreneur! Remember, failure is part of the adventure.

STEP 2: What will people pay you for?

You've noted the things that sound interesting to you? Good! Now go through that list again. This time, think about which of those you think you could find people to pay you for.

Focus on stuff that you can productise – which is a fancy, businessy way of saying 'stuff you can resell over and over again'. It's much easier to sell a copy of the same T-shirt 100 times than to sell 100 unique T-shirts one time. It's much easier to build three similar websites than to build three very different ones.

Identify one to three options that you think would be easiest to sell, and we'll focus on them for the rest of this chapter.

THE BEST AGE TO START BABYSITTING OR AU PAIRING

Babysitting or au pairing is often the first job young people do, but this is something best left to your later teens, when you are mature enough to look after someone else on your own. Also, do you know that young kids can be TERRIFYING – how can such tiny humans produce so many weird body fluids, I ask you?! If you're going to try babysitting, you should skill up with a First Aid course through your school or another organisation first, so that you're fully ready for the responsibility.

If you're going to do something like entertaining kids during holidays with crafting/art activities/adventure games, you can get around the responsibility thing by insisting that you run the event at one of the parents' houses, or at your own house while your parents are there.

STREAMING, VLOGGING AND THAT INFLUENCER LIFE

You've probably heard of kids who have made millions becoming game streamers or vloggers or social media influencers. It seems like the ideal side-hustle, right? Just film yourself talking about what you love and have people send you free stuff and pay you for it!

Unfortunately, the reality isn't always so glamorous. Streaming and vlogging can be dangerous: people get harassed and bullied online, and sometimes this even turns into real-life stalking. There are a lot of creeps out there.

These careers are also really competitive – most people who try this out will spend a lot of time and effort making content that doesn't get seen. It can still be really fun to make content for the internet. I should know, I've started like thirty different podcasts/vlogs/blogs over the years (and made a grand total of R0 from them). It can be a great hobby, but don't expect it to make you millions, and be aware of the risks.

If you want to try this route, I wish you luck, but please make sure that an adult knows what you're doing so they can support you if things turn mean. Also, lock down your private security online.[36] And remember that, technically, you aren't allowed to use a lot of these platforms until you're at least 13.[37]

LEARNING TO PRICE YOUR PRODUCTS PROFITABLY

A profit means how much money you get for your business, minus all the costs of that business.

Say you want to start a side-hustle selling vegan brownies at R20 each, and the ingredients for each brownie will cost you R8. You'll make R12 profit on each brownie.

But there might be more costs than that. Maybe your big

36 Here are some great instructions for how to do that: http://www.crashoverridenetwork.com/coach.html

37 I know I sound like a killjoy about this, but I literally know YouTube stars who've had to leave their homes and go into hiding because people got so cruel and weird. Please be safe.

brother's boyfriend offers to take your brownies to his university classes (where EVERYONE is a vegan)[38] and sell them there for you, but he wants R50 each time he does this for you, no matter how many brownies he sells. How many brownies do you need to sell before you start making a profit, now? (Psst . . . in this example, it would be 50 ÷ 12 = 4.2, so round it up, and you've got to sell 5 brownies before you start making a profit.)

Even services can have costs. Say you want to wash cars for your neighbours. Will you need to buy your own soap and bucket? And you've got to think about your time as having a cost, too. If you have to spend five hours just to make R10, that's not a very profitable side-hustle, because you could have been using that valuable time to do something WAY more fun like playing fetch with your local squirrels.

So, let's go back to your side-hustle ideas, and figure out which ones might be profitable. You don't have to get fancy about this – just grab a calculator, a pen and a piece of paper, and let's work out how much you'd need to sell your products for so you can make a profit.

LET'S WORK OUT THREE THINGS

- What price you can sell your products or services for
- What it will cost you to make them
- Calculate the profit

Let's do this exercise now, to work out if you've got a profitable side-hustle idea on your hands.

---

38 Don't make fun – I'm a vegan too! I blame my mom for making me be friends with so many animals when I was a kid.

STEP 1: Price

The best way to figure out what price you can put on a product or a service is to research what other people are charging for a similar thing (ideally, in the same place as you want to sell your product or service).

You can get away with a slightly higher price if you're more convenient. Say you're selling bags of chips to the crowd at a sports game for R2 more than your customers could get them at the shop down the road: they're probably going to pay the extra R2 to you because you're right there, so they don't have to miss some of the game walking to the shops.

So do some research about what other people charge for products like yours. If you want to offer a service, ask around for party entertainment, dog-walking rates or jobbing rates. Ask family members and friends what they already pay others. Look at the community notices at the library or your local shop. Go look around on the internet for people offering the same kind of product or service you're trying to offer, and see what the going prices are.

STEP 2: Costs

Write down all the costs that will go into your side-hustle. Remember to include:

- Ingredients/materials/equipment
- Letting people know about your business (stuff like printing posters)
- Transport

Do some research and estimate what everything will cost you. If you can save money by buying cheaper materials (without losing quality), then you must absolutely do that.

Shop around and get the best prices for the ingredients. You'll make more profit if your costs are lower.

STEP 3: Profit

Calculate the difference and that is your profit (remember: price – cost = profit).

Bear in mind that how profitable a side-hustle is isn't the only measure of whether it's worth your time. For a large chunk of my 20s, I earned more every hour I spent being the world's clumsiest waitress than at my actual 9-to-5 day job, but I knew that day job was teaching me skills that would one day make my time way more valuable. If you think this side-hustle will teach you valuable skills, then go for it, even if it won't make you much money now.

THINK BIG

The smart way to make a side-hustle more profitable is to think bigger, because most things get cheaper to make when you sell more of them.

Here's an example. Let's imagine that you want to start a side-hustle making emoji cakes, and that you'll charge R100 per cake. Here are the ingredients you need to make one cake:[39]

- 120 g flour
- 120 g castor sugar
- 120 g butter
- 2 eggs

---

39 I'm terrible at baking so please don't actually try this recipe. It would probably come out tasting like the poop emoji, know what I mean?

But the thing is, you can't buy a 120 g bag of flour from the closest shop. You can only buy a 1 kg bag of flour, which costs R12. Here's what else you'd have to buy:

FOR 1 CAKE

You need	You can buy	It will cost
120 g flour	1 kg flour	R12
120 g castor sugar	500 g castor sugar	R22
120 g butter	500 g butter	R60
2 eggs	6 eggs	R22
	TOTAL	**R116**

That one cake is going to cost you R116. If you sold that one cake for R100, you'd have LOST R16. But the thing is, after making that cake, you'll have enough ingredients left to make another two cakes. So if you sold three cakes, they'd each cost you 116 ÷ 3 = R39 each. You'd make R184 profit. Much better!

But hey, what if you go even bigger? If you make 20 cakes, you can buy the ingredients in bulk, which means they'll be even cheaper. Here are the prices I came up with, by looking at what I could buy from my local supermarket:

FOR 20 CAKES

You need	You can buy	It will cost
120 g × 20 = 2.4 kg flour	2.5 kg flour	R23
120 g × 20 = 2.4 kg castor sugar	3 kg castor sugar	R96
120 g × 20 = 2.4 kg butter	2.5 kg butter	R300
2 × 20 = 40 eggs	48 eggs	R87
	TOTAL	**R506**

So, 20 cakes would cost you R506 to make, which works out to about R25 per cake! You'd make R1 494. AND you'd have ingredients left over. Now we're talking . . . 😋🐶😸💜😊🐾🍰

Thinking big works for services, too. If you can have several customers you're charging for the same hour of work, you can end up doubling, tripling or quadrupling your money. So, if you run a morning crafts event for five-year-olds and have only one kid at a charge of R25 each, you'd make R25. Have three kids there, and you will make R75, and it will take you the same amount of time. THAT's how you think smart, and really make your side-hustle start spinning cash.

> ### Adding value
>
> A great thing about being an entrepreneur is that you'll be learning practically about a money concept I find pretty fascinating: that one way to make money grow (apart from interest) is to add value – in other words, to create something that is worth more than it cost to make. A cake is worth more than the ingredients that went into it. If you can add value to something, you are literally making money. Hold on to this idea! It's an interesting one.

FINDING CUSTOMERS

Having the most amazing emoji cakes/dog-walking service/vegan brownies in the world isn't worth anything unless you find some customers.

There are two main ways you can do that: by going to where your customers are, or by bringing your customers to you.

Going to your customers

- You're probably going to want to start off in your neighbourhood (like setting up a lemonade stall outside your house, or selling fudge at a local shop) or selling in places where you aren't charged much to have a stall. Selling locally to friends and neighbours can also be a really good way of checking whether the quality of what you are selling is good enough (ask your MEAN friends, because it's better to know sooner rather than later).

- Look out for markets, fun days or events in your area that are specifically geared towards kid entrepreneurs. There are a couple that run during school holidays.

- If an adult you know runs a business, ask them if they can sell your product there (but be prepared to accept a 'no' if it doesn't work for them). This works well if they run a related business. I have a friend who runs a coffee-roasting business. He sells coffee from a van. His son has been selling home-made biscuits from the van since he was six – and he is now 16.

- Think about transport. How can you get around the fact that you can't get everywhere? Can you use others to sell for you at the places they go to? If you make muffins, perhaps there are people at your mother's workplace and your grandma's stokvel who will place a regular order.

- If you are making crafts, ask the adult in your life to help you research local online marketplaces like Hello Pretty, Kamers and Mzansi Marketplace. You can only sell like this if your products are really excellent. But do think of going this way, because there are some reputable providers out there who can help you to reach a wider audience and make money while you sleep. You'll need someone over 18 to open an account or profile at the online marketplace. Remember to check the costs associated with selling, such as commission and finance charges for sales. But really, this is only for really excellent products, so maybe hold off until you have tested your products in the real world first.

Bringing customers to you

- Post about your products on your local Facebook neighbourhood group.
- Make pamphlets or posters. There are brilliant easy-to-use online design apps, like Canva, that can help you design really fabulous marketing material (you can also use these apps to design products like cards). You need to get permission to put up your posters in public places such as parks and schools, but lots of shops and libraries have community notice boards where you can advertise. Don't forget to add the cost of printing to your product costs.
- Make giveaways – tiny samples of your brownies that you hand out on toothpicks at the local shop or a recording of you reading a fun-filled story to younger kids that your folks and clients can post on their social media accounts.
- If you are running a service, get a testimonial from every single client in the early days. Just ask – most people will help you. You'll need these testimonials later.
- Get your first customers to refer you to your next customers. If they won't, then this probably isn't your side-hustle. That's okay, that's why we made a long list! Move on to your next option.

- Later: Once you're sure you've got a product, it's really quick and easy to set up a website these days using something like Squarespace or Wix. Put all those testimonials on it (if you do this well enough, you can get people to pay you to make websites for them, as a whole other side-hustle).
- Later: Once your business is really ready to take off, find a free course on online marketing (Google AdWords is a good place to start, but apps like Instagram can also be good places to advertise your products) and sell yo' stuff, lovelies.

Talking to people (about yourself and your products)

You know how your folks always taught you never to talk to strangers? Well, when you're starting a side-hustle, that's exactly what you're going to have to learn how to do. In any business, it's really important to be able to talk to people in a friendly and interested way. It's a great skill to have in life, generally.

If you are meeting someone, remember to greet them and introduce yourself by name. Smile. Be polite. Ask for their permission to talk to them about your product – it's rude to try to sell something to someone who's busy doing something else.

If you are selling a product or service, work out what you can say about it before you try to sell it to people. Practise talking about it, with anyone who will let you use them as your guinea pig.

Be genuinely interested in helping people. That means asking them questions to find out about what they're looking for. If they are looking for something that you don't have, don't try to 'hard sell' your product. Rather, help them find what they want (if you have this information) and wish them a nice day!

STAYING SAFE WHILE YOU SIDE-HUSTLE

As a general rule, you should run your side-hustle ideas past your folks before you start trying them. They'll be able to spot potential issues and help you brainstorm ways to side-hustle safely. Every community is different, so I can't give you general rules about what will be safe where you are. You know who can, though? Your folks!

Your folks can also help you see problems that you might not think about, and figure out what you'll do about them, like what happens if someone's dog attacks the dog you are walking. They can help you to work out what you need to agree with customers about terms and conditions (like they are responsible if their dog misbehaves, or if their dog is actually an alien in disguise and it beams back up to its home world mid-walk). They might have to help you with transport. Getting their buy-in is a no-brainer!

Some other important things to think about: be careful giving out your address or full name when you advertise. Ask for payment (at least half of the amount) before you hand over the goods or finish the service. Ask for your folks to accompany you the first time you meet a client, to make sure they're not dodgy. And always trust your instincts.

There's no such thing as free money
When you're looking for a side-hustle, be careful of scams. One of the most common types of scams is called a pyramid scheme. Here's how a pyramid scheme works:

- You join the scheme by paying some money in.

- You're then told to recruit other people into the scheme. They all pay money in, too.
- When new recruits pay money in, you get a cut of their money. Most of it goes to the person who recruited you, and the person who recruited them, and so on.

In other words, the scheme only 'makes money' by getting new recruits in, all the time. Eventually, the scheme collapses because it's trying to grow exponentially (remember the rats on the ship?) but there are no more people to be recruited. The faster a pyramid scheme grows, the faster this will happen. The person at the top of the pyramid makes a fortune. Most other people lose almost everything.

number of participants

levels

1.
6
36
216
1 296
7 776
46 656
279 936
1 679 616
10 077 696
60 466 176 → MORE THAN POPULATION OF SOUTH AFRICA
362 797 056
2,176 782 336
13, 060 694 016

2.
3.
4.
5.
6.
7.
8.
9.
10.
11.
12.
13.

→ MORE THAN THE WORLD POPULATION

Multilevel marketing schemes are just pyramid schemes with better branding. They try to disguise their true nature by pretending to sell a 'product', but 90% of the emphasis is on selling a 'business opportunity' to . . . you guessed it . . . sell those products to other people. So, you've got to ask yourself, who's actually buying the products? Only people buying them to sell to other people, who are . . . selling them to other people to sell to other people? See the problem?

These things are the devil. Avoid them at all costs.

There's one major rule to help you avoid scams: if it sounds too good to be true, it probably is.

Things to look out for:

- Scams only offer complicated payment methods like Bitcoin. This often means their bank accounts have been frozen.
- It's hard to get a clear answer when you ask them questions about their business model.
- Scams sell a product, but mostly they're trying to convince you to start selling a product, too.

If you're ever unsure about whether something is a scam, check it out on www.scam.com. You can also check whether the company has a registration number with the Financial Services Board or the National Stokvel Association of South Africa. And, if you're still not sure, just assume it's a scam.

MAKING A PLAN

Let's wrap up everything you learnt in this chapter by putting together a plan for ACTION! Here's a basic business plan that you might want to work through, to think about all the things you need to do to get your side-hustle off the ground.

What's your product/service?	
COSTS	**PRICE AND PROFIT**
What materials/equipment/ingredients will you need for your business?	What can you charge for each ONE of your products or services?
Where will you buy them?	How much do you need to sell before you start making a profit?
How much will they cost?	Are there ways that you can think bigger, to make more profit?
	How will you decide if your side-hustle is a success?

Plan

How will you find customers?

How much time will you need?

How will you keep records of your costs and your profit?

What do you need to do next?

Tax on your side-hustles

Income tax is money all South Africans pay to the government, from money they earn. The nice thing is that you don't have to pay any income tax at all if you earn less than R80 000-ish a year. I'm assuming you won't be making that much.

If you are, SHEESH, okay, this book has nothing to teach you. Also, you'll need to go register with the South African Revenue Service (SARS, the taxman) and get someone to help you complete a tax return.

IN SUMMARY!

- Everybody should have a side-hustle, because chances are there will be at least one time in your adult life when you'll need to, or you'll want to, run your own business. NOW is the best time to practise doing this, because failure doesn't matter.
- The best side-hustles use unique skills you have, or help you **develop** the skills you **want** to have.
- To make more of a profit, you can find cheaper ingredients/materials, or think big to reduce your costs.
- Safety first when you side-hustle!

Chapter 7
YOUR FUTURE CAREER

WHAT DO YOU WANT TO BE WHEN YOU GROW UP?

The weirdest question in the world is, 'What do you want to be when you grow up?' For one thing, why is it about what you want to BE rather than what you want to DO? (Can I answer, 'I'd like to be a twelve-tentacled space monster with laser eyes'?) You will be many different things over the course of your life. You'll be a friend and a son or daughter. You'll be a citizen of your country and a member of many communities. You might be some kind of artist or athlete (whether you get paid to do this or not). You will probably be someone's employee, and someone's boss. You might be a parent or a pet-parent. You might be an activist. You will probably be someone's hero, someone's teacher, someone's partner in crime. There will be times when you'll be a lazy slob! So, when people ask this question, it's weird that they're really just talking about one aspect of who you are: what job you'll have.

And even *that's* a weird question, because most people will have *many* jobs over their lifetimes, especially people from your generation.

People treat this question of what job you want to do like it's something you'll answer only once when you're, like, 21 (the mythical time 'when you're grown up') and that's the answer for the rest of your life. It isn't. It's a question you're going to need to answer every day until you die.

So here's my advice to you: don't stress so much about what you want to 'be' when you grow up. Rather, focus on **honing your skills**. Focus on what you **can do**. Find something you like doing, and practise doing it until you're good at it. If those skills are rare, that's even better.

The funny thing about skills is that they can be applied to all sorts of different jobs. You might become really good at accounting, but then end up running a theatre, or be the director of a climate-change activist group, or work for the police helping them to track down criminals, because it turns out that accounting is an important skill for all of those jobs. When you're young, focus on your skills, so that later, once you're clearer about the problems in the world that you really care about fixing, you'll have some pretty powerful tools that you can use to fix them.

Having skills is better than having a plan for your life, because how can you plan for the future when you have no idea what the future will be? Deng Xiaoping, a really smart dude, called this life strategy 'crossing the river by feeling the stones'. The more skills you have, the more stones there are for you to find. Skills give you **options**.

You might not have your first real job for many years still. But **skills** are things that you're developing now. Cristiano Ronaldo joined his first soccer team when he was 7. Beyoncé joined her first singing group at 9. Richard Branson started his first business at 16. If you want to be great at something, now is the best time to start doing it.

And do you want to know the best way to develop your skills? Start a side-hustle!

You all know how I love lists. So, make one now. What are all your skills? What things can you do better than most people? Write down everything:

- People skills, like 'I can defuse tense arguments really well' or 'All grandmothers love me for some reason'.
- Technical skills, like 'I can take great photographs' or 'I have an intricate knowledge of the inside of a Raspberry PI computer'.
- Stuff you know about, like 'I can quote every line of dialogue from all seven seasons of *Buffy the Vampire Slayer*' (this is me, by the way) or 'I can tell you everything about every type of dinosaur that ever existed'.
- Stuff you are good at because you do it for fun, like 'I can knit beanies' or 'I can make up brilliant party games' or 'I know how to walk dogs'.

Next to each skill, add two more columns:

- On a scale of 1–3, how easy will it be to make money out of this? Is it highly valued by society?
- On a scale of 1–3, how much do I enjoy doing this thing?

Now, star one or two of these skills that are high 3s. Focus on honing those skills even more. This exercise helps you figure out what you want to focus on becoming great at, but it's also a good way to start building a clear narrative about what you're good at, to tell other people.

Think broadly; don't limit yourself. I legit know a guy who's a prominent international sports commentator for the video game StarCraft.

Return to this list every couple of months for the next few years and you will be amazed at what you can do.

MONEY AND HAPPINESS

You know how people say that money can't buy happiness? I'm going to say something controversial: those people are wrong! There is a clear relationship between how much money you have and how happy you are. But that relationship is more complicated than you may think.

Researchers have spent a lot of time studying whether money makes us happy.[40] They affirm that money definitely does make you happier, but the relationship looks like this:

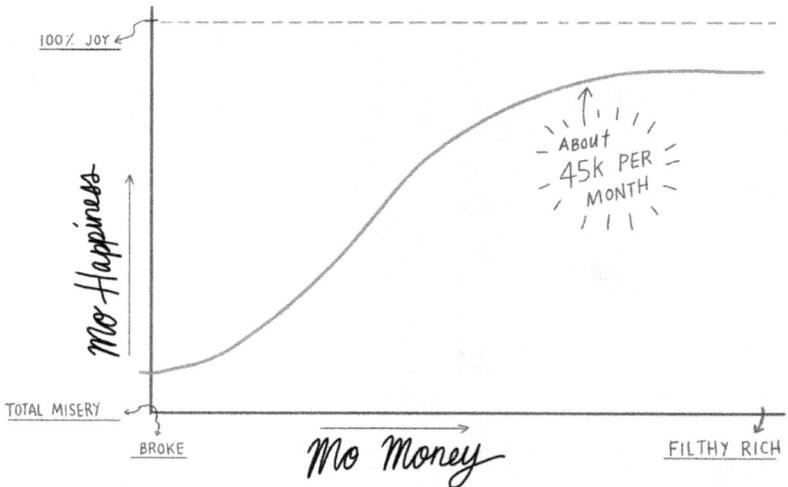

Not having enough money is very stressful. If you don't have enough money, you can't buy food, you can't access good healthcare, you can't find a safe and comfortable place to live. So, if you give an extra R1 000 a month to someone who's poor, that's going to make a huge difference in their life. Give the same R1 000 to someone who's rich, and it will barely register.

40 Thanks, https://80000hours.org/articles/money-and-happiness, for the excellent summary.

And beyond a certain level, more money doesn't really make you noticeably happier. In South Africa, I calculate that number to be about R45 000 a month before tax.[41] But that's right at the top of the curve, where more money makes basically NO difference. Even below that number, if you're earning R20 000 or R25 000 a month, other things start to matter far more than money, like your health, relationships and a sense of purpose.

Money can buy **some** happiness, or to be more specific: NOT having enough money increases the chances that you'll be stressed and worried. But there's also a **real limit** to how much happiness money can buy.

So what this means is: your goal in life DOES NOT need for you to be the richest person on the block. That goal is going to make it difficult to do some of the things you might really want to do (and it will make you a pretty boring person). Your goal can be more modest – to make as much as you need to live freely, and a little bit more if you want to. And this target really is something that you can achieve, as an adult – but only if you get into the right habits now, while you are young.

Some kids are literally researching which jobs make the most money, and then basing future study and work plans on that. I don't think that's a great way to live a happy life. What I think is, sure, find out what you can expect to earn in different careers,[42] and be realistic about the careers that

41 You should know, that's much more than most South Africans earn every month.

42 You can do some internet research on this. I found a great infographic at on the Educonnect website https://3mi2wy3arf4n3ge2uzb86do3-wp-engine.netdna-ssl.com/wp-content/uploads/2017/08/how-much-do-professionals-earn-infographic.pdf

will make it hard for you to earn enough money. Choose a career that will give you financial stability as well as joy and meaning, and try to learn some well-paid skills as a backup.[43] But don't discard a possibility just because it earns less. Rather ask, can I earn **enough**? As long as you earn enough, and save, you are on your path to wealth.

> What are your five best memories of the past year?
> Talk to your folks: what are the five things that they did for you that they spent the most money on in the past year?
> How many things are on both lists?

WHY SOME JOBS EARN MORE THAN OTHERS

There is a BIG gap between what some types of jobs earn and what others do.

Job	Average monthly income (before tax)
Cashier	R4 000
Security guard	R5 000
Low-level police officer	R12 000
Electrician	R14 000
Government-school teacher	R15 000
Secretary	R16 000

43 I have always wanted to write books, but when I learnt what average full-time authors earn for a living, I decided that I needed other skills on top of writing. I'm really glad that I learnt skills like how to make apps and how to write code, so that I could earn enough money to support my very expensive book-writing habit.

Job	Average monthly income (before tax)
Graphic designer	R18 000
Software developer	R38 000
Pharmacist	R48 000
Building foreman	R53 000
Financial analyst	R58 000
Senior university lecturer	R70 000
Dentist	R110 000
Lawyer	R160 000
Partner in a top law firm	R200 000
Government minister	R210 000
The South African president	R260 000
Top company CEOs	R2 million – R8 million

Note: Except where I've indicated, these are the average salaries for intermediate positions in each field (usually people with about five to ten years' experience).[44]

Why do some jobs earn so much money, and others earn so little? There are lots of different factors.

The first part of this is about your skills. If your skills are difficult to get, require years of study and are rare, you'll probably earn more for them. But that's not always true. It takes as long to train to become a scientist as to become a lawyer, but most lawyers get paid more than most scientists.

The second part is about **how many employers want this skill, versus how many people there are who are competing for that job**. There are thousands of unemployed BCom graduates in South Africa, but the government is

---

[44] I've compiled these from a number of sources, but the best summary is this one: https://www.careerjunction.co.za/marketing/salarysurvey

literally handing out visas to people from other countries because certain critical skills are impossible to find locally. You can find a link to this list of skills on the website. It includes unglamorous but fascinating professions like forestry technicians, geologists and protein scientists.

Salaries are also linked to **economic growth** in particular fields. Economic growth happens when the value of the goods and services in a particular field increases. If there is growth in your industry, such as IT, you will earn more than someone in an industry where there is no growth, such as construction. Businesses in the industry can afford to pay you more, and want to pay you more, because you are making more money for them. That's why in South Africa an architect is currently earning less than a software developer, for example, even though they studied for the same amount of time. You really, REALLY want to be developing skills in areas where there's a lot of economic growth. Imagine the person who got really good at fixing horse-drawn carriages after the car was invented. I bet he was MAD.

It also matters how much power employees have in an industry versus the businesses. Industries with strong unions are usually able to negotiate better salaries for their employees. An industry dominated by one or two big companies usually doesn't have to pay much, because there's nowhere else for their employees to go if they're unhappy. In some sectors, salaries are also affected by what the government pays. Salaries for teachers and nurses are very much set by the government, because the government is the biggest employer. Of course, governments are voted in by society, so in a sense that reflects how people in society value those jobs. In some countries teachers are highly paid, and highly valued. Maybe that will happen here one day too!

The best way to have more power as an employee is to be your own boss. An electrician who works for someone else is going to make much less money than an electrician who starts her own business.

RANGES OF INCOME

It's important to remember that looking at the **average income** for a career doesn't tell you the whole story. Some industries have a large range of incomes, and others have a small range.

Being a government minister has a small income range, because every minister gets paid the same. There's only one employer (the government), and they have to pay everyone the same amount.

Being a musician, on the other hand, has a HUGE range. The average musician's salary is a GREAT BIG ROUND ZERO: think about every person who sings at their church on Sundays or plays drums on weekends. The guy who sits outside the local shopping centre playing guitar probably isn't making much money, either. Or, you know, you could be Beyoncé, who earns an average income of R193 918 087 a month.

In most professions, you can earn much more than the average person if you become one of the best in your field.

Incomes of the rich and famous

- *Cosmopolitan* magazine calculates that Trevor Noah earned R425 000 000 a year between June 2018 and June 2019 – he is the fourth-highest-paid stand-up comedian in Hollywood.

- Charlize Theron is the ninth-highest-paid actress in the world, with an estimated income of R27 558 983 a month in 2019.
- Siya Kolisi's average salary should fall between R50 000 and R69 375 per month, which is the estimated annual salary of South African rugby players – but this excludes any bonuses for wins. And because he is a top player, he probably earns much more than that, because of sponsorships and advertising deals.

IS UNIVERSITY WORTH IT?

University is expensive and it takes a long time. Is it worth it?

The short answer, in South Africa, is **yes**. In South Africa, 55 % of young people (under 25) with matric are unemployed, compared to 31 % of young people with a university degree. People with university degrees will also earn more over their lifetimes, on average, than people without degrees (and that gap is bigger in our country than in some other countries).

That said, university's not the only way to be a success in life, and it's not for everyone. Be sure that it's the right route for you before you commit to it. The university dropout rate in South Africa is really high: about 50 %. It shoots up way higher for students who attempt distance-learning degrees at institutions like Unisa. So a lot of people are taking out student loans and never getting the degree that might make the loans worthwhile.

Before you think about financing a university education, do your homework. Find out what the throughput rate is at that particular institution (the percentage of people who register in first year and end up graduating). Have a clear idea of how your degree will improve your life – and be smart about what you choose to study.

Once you're sure you're ready to commit to a university degree, you've got a few options for funding:[45]

- National Student Financial Aid Scheme (NSFAS) loans: This is a government organisation, so the repayment terms are fair and up to 40% of the loan can be converted into a bursary if you do well enough. The NSFAS should always be the first thing you try, but bear in mind that they have strict deadlines.
- Bursaries and special loans: Most universities publish a list of specific bursaries and special loans that are available for their institution, often focusing on specific religious or identity groups, or degrees. Talk to the financial-aid office at the institution to which you're applying.
- If you're studying an in-demand degree, approach the big companies who hire people with that degree. They often have special bursary and loan funds and may also employ you after you graduate.

If none of those options work, you can consider a private loan. There's a company called Fundi that specialises in student loans, and most of the banks also offer this kind of lending. If you need a private loan, approach every institution and get a quote from each of them. Compare their terms and find the loan with the best interest rate and most generous repayment terms. There's also a new platform called Feenix, which allows students to crowdfund their degrees through donations.

---

45 I'm writing this whole section at a time when fees have not yet fallen completely, but huge changes have been promised. Forgive me if a lot of this goes out of date very soon.

OTHER TERTIARY OPTIONS

Universities have basically been teaching exactly the same way for hundreds of years. Recently, there has been a global move towards experimenting with more hands-on tertiary learning styles, which work more like structured apprenticeships than like classrooms.

South Africa has a long and proud tradition of technical and vocational education and training (TVET) colleges – institutions that focus on practical and hands-on skills training that leads to diplomas rather than university degrees. There are about 50 registered TVET colleges all around the country. As with universities, their quality can vary, so do your homework and find out what their throughput rate is. Also ask them to show you statistics of postgraduate employment.

TVET students can also apply for funding from the NSFAS.

Locally, there is a whole bunch of really interesting new private institutions to take a look at, like Project codeX and WeThinkCode, both of which offer a way to learn to become a software developer in a hands-on environment, and both of which are very cheap or free for students. We are going to need a lot more coders over the next few decades to help us prepare for the war against the robots, so consider this route.

The unfathomably wonderful thing about living in the new millennium is that you can literally access the best lectures by the smartest people in the world while sitting at home in your underpants. You can take Harvard's entire first-year Computer Science course on the internet, for free. You can go to YouTube and watch a video that will teach you how to build a solar panel using things you can buy at the hardware store. We live in the future, and it's amazing.

There are opportunities to learn all around you, if you're

motivated enough to find them. You can find online courses for literally anything these days, often for free, or for just a few hundred rand a month. Often, if you pay a small amount, you can also get a certificate confirming that you've completed the course.

We live in a complex world. Learning, for your generation, is something that you're never going to stop doing. You're going to have to find ways to learn well, and learn cheaply, and to make learning fun. Luckily, there have never been more options for you.

This is a good time to have another chat with your folks: are they saving up for you to go to university? If they can't, can you all work out a plan together so that you can start a side-hustle and save up by yourself?

FUTURE-PROOF YOUR CAREER

The job fields with the most growth in South Africa in 2018 and 2019 were in software/IT, finance and engineering, and those kinds of jobs are very well paid – good news for those of you with a bent for maths and science.[46] But more and more, research is showing that, as the global business environment changes because of advances in technology, people with the ability to innovate and be creative, work well in teams (understand other people and what they are trying to do), and communicate well are going to be the key to creating growth in industries. So those of you with skills in

---

46 https://businesstech.co.za/news/business/305576/these-are-the-best-
    earning-professions-in-south-africa/

those areas – often those of you who love history, geography, languages and the arts – might want to look at how you can use those to up your earning potential.

Currently in South Africa, petroleum engineers who work on turning coal into energy are very highly paid. Won't that change as the demand for green energy increases, and people with the ability to imagine alternative technologies are needed? Already some of those technologies are taking over, in countries that are committed to lowering emissions.

As the world changes, the world of work will keep changing. Many of you reading this book will have jobs that don't exist yet.[47] So don't worry too much if you don't know what you want to do when you're older. Just keep working on those skills, and you'll be ready for those opportunities when they arise.

IN SUMMARY!

- It's fine if you have no idea which job you want one day. You'll probably have many different jobs! For now, rather focus on building your skills.
- Build up some skills that are paid well, but know that being super-rich probably won't make you any happier than just earning **enough**.
- University is awesome, and there are lots of different ways to fund it. But if it's not for you, there are loads of other options, too.
- The world is full of possibilities, and I'm so excited for you to explore as many of them as you can!

---

47 My partner works for a company that builds surgery robots. The future is weird.

PART 3

MASTERING

MONEY

Chapter 8

ENVELOPES ARE BETTER THAN BUDGETS

Have you ever been bowling? I'm terrible at bowling. I have to put up the walls on the sides of the lane that make it impossible for you to get a gutter ball. Yes, I do this even though I AM 33 YEARS OLD. I want you to have a gutter-ball protector for your money. A system that makes life **easy** for you. The equivalent of a gutter-ball protector for money is what we call the **envelope**.

Envelopes . . . you know . . . those things people used to put letters into in the olden days. Imagine you had a pile of cash, and you put it inside different envelopes. And each of those envelopes had a label: one of the envelopes was for buying Lego, another was money you plan to give to charity. Now, when you go to the Lego store, you only take the envelope

labelled LEGO MONEY, and you definitely do NOT bring the envelope labelled MONEY FOR CHARITY. That way, there's no chance you'll accidentally spend too much money on a fully functional Lego model of the Millennium Falcon and not have any money left to donate.

Now, compare envelopes to another way you might have heard of for managing money: a budget. A budget is where you write down a list of how you plan to spend your money. It would look something like this:

Toiletries	R100
Uber	R100
Clothes	R250
Eating out and movies	R200
Airtime	R150
Money for charity	R200
TOTAL	**R1 000**

See, that's nice and all, but if you have the whole R1 000 sitting in your pocket when you go to the Lego shop, you can be sure that money is going to be whispering in your ear . . . *spend meeeeee* . . . and your plan is going to go right out the window.[48]

Budgeting doesn't work because you are not the perfectly rational, long-term planning creature you pretend you are. You are a primate with pants on.

We all have good intentions, but your brain is not a perfect computer that follows the instructions you give it. Your brain did not evolve to handle modern life where, at any one time, there are six billion fun things you could be doing and

---

48 Trust me, and my enormous Lego collection.

an endless supply of food you could be eating and *She-Ra* episodes to be watching, except you shouldn't be doing those things because of some vague future where you'll regret being broke/unhealthy/failing school. Your brain evolved to want shiny stuff it can have NOW more than important stuff it can have in the future.

Remember this: your brain evolved to help you find berries in the jungle, not to resist all the temptations of modern life.

So, really, it's quite ridiculous to expect that some system where you tell yourself, 'Okay, brain, I'm going to parade a thousand extremely delicious-looking marshmallows in front of your face, and you're just going to resist every single one of them,' is a good system. It's a stupid system. Your brain is stupid and you've got to understand it and be kind to it and work within its limitations, not try to fight it.

So, what if, instead of this budget, had just three envelopes labelled . . .

- FUN MONEY – R600
- BASICS – R200
- MONEY FOR CHARITY – R200

. . . and you only put one week's worth of fun money in your wallet at a time?

Doesn't that seem like an easier system to deal with?

Your envelopes don't have to be real, paper envelopes, either. You could have different bank accounts, where you split up your money. That's what I do: I have a bank account for my day-to-day fun money, a bank account for my grownup bills, and an account for big stuff I'm saving up for.

Or you could try having a system that's half cash and half bank account. I have a friend who keeps all his money in a bank account, and he draws the money that he wants to spend as cash. He's in the habit of never swiping his bank card unless it's an emergency or a really big transaction.

You've got to outsmart your own monkey brain. You do that by putting your money in envelopes, so you can protect yourself from your own worst impulses.

When we put our money in envelopes (real or virtual), we're giving every rand a job to do. We're saying to this one rand, 'Your job is to buy me lunch,' and another rand, 'Your job is to buy me something fun!' That means you're not spending your money mindlessly – you're putting it to work making your life better (or making the world better). It's a wonderful feeling of control.

You don't need to plan on a rand-by-rand level, though. It can be helpful to think in percentage rules, like: 'I'll give 10% of my money to charity, save half of the rest, and spend what's left,' or 'One third for savings, one third for fun and one third for buying sensible things.' There are a lot of different rule systems that work for different people. You've got to find the right envelope system for you, and the right set of rules to go with it.

Stop and think about what your main envelopes are. You might want to include envelopes like this:

Fun Money (money you want to spend now, on stuff like fashion, going out, hobbies, gifts, etc.).

Basics (if you're responsible for buying some of the basics you need, like clothes or data or toiletries, you might want an envelope for that).

Savings (saving for specific, bigger goals that you want to buy, like maybe you're saving up for a game console or for a car).

Freedom Fund (saving money to build wealth for

yourself, so that you've got more options to do whatever you want to do with your life later – this is usually money that would be invested).

Money for Charity or tithing (money you want to donate to a cause you feel strongly about).

I recommend that you don't have more than five envelopes, but your envelopes might look different from these ones.

Now, think about how you'll allocate money to these envelopes. Here's a starting suggestion:

Basics: 30%

Fun Money: 20%

Savings: 20%

Freedom Fund: 20%

Charity: 10%

If that's too complicated, you could also try a very simple three-part system I like:

One third for spending

One third for saving

One third for giving

Some people who get an allowance but also have some side-hustles like to allocate their money like this:

Allowance money is for spending

Side-hustle money is for saving

Plus 10% of ALL money goes to charity

That might not be the right plan for you! Allocating money is a very personal thing, and you're the only one who knows what will be the right plan for your life. But take some time now, and think about how you want YOUR plan to look.

My envelopes are:	This envelope will get this much of my money (as a percentage):

CASH OR CARD?

It's a good idea to practise your envelope system with cash for a couple of months, to get the hang of it. That's because working with cold, hard fistfuls of cash feels more real to our monkey brains than swiping a bank card (plus, holding a stack of cash makes you feel like a celebrity). When you're working with cash, get some actual envelopes from a stationery store and use them for sorting your money. You'll also need to buy a small notebook that you keep with you. When you spend money, write down in your little notebook what you spent each day, and any money you earned, like this:

Monday 14 January – Coke and chips from the tuck shop: –R15.50
Wednesday 16 January – extra money for washing Grandma's car: + R30
Thursday 17 January – cat toys: –R80

Once you've got the hang of this, it's a good idea to ask your folks to help you open a real bank account.

Bank accounts keep your money safer than walking around with cash, and let you do more complex types of transactions like recurring payments. They also will keep a record of where all your money goes, so you don't have to write down everything you spend (which gets really old, really fast).

There are different types of accounts:

- **A current account/cheque account/transactional account:** These are all just ways of saying 'a normal bank account for day-to-day spending money'. The account will come with a bank card, and you can also make payments from an app or online banking. You normally pay a fee to have an account like this, and don't get paid interest on money in this account.
- **A savings account:** An account that pays you interest on your money. Sometimes, these accounts also have a bank card attached to them, but most don't.
- **A combination account:** Some banks have started offering a combined account where you get a bank card and can swipe it at the shops like a transactional account, but they ALSO offer you interest on your savings. My two favourite accounts like this are the Capitec Global One account and the Old Mutual Money account, but check out the website for an up-to-date list (stuff like this changes a lot).

I like to have two different transactional accounts (one for Fun Money, one for Basics) and a separate savings account. It's easiest to open different accounts at the same bank. Capitec offers cheap and easy bank accounts, and lets you open five different envelopes, so it's a great starter account.

Being with the same bank as your folks is a good idea, because if they send money to you, it will arrive more quickly. But don't stress too much about choosing the perfect bank account – they're all pretty similar.

Some people say that you should stay with the same bank your whole life, so that one day when you want a home loan, they're more likely to give it to you. That's not how it works any more. It's not like there's a nice ou toppie who's the bank manager, who knows you by name and who's going to personally suss you out. Computers make these decisions now. And computers don't understand loyalty. Remember this when the robot uprising happens.

> Once you've got the hang of enveloping with cash, ask your folks to help you open your own bank account.

MONEY MISSION CONTROL

You know how in movies about astronauts there are a bunch of people sitting back home in a control room, watching a bunch of screens where they can track the spaceship's every move? That room is called MISSION CONTROL, and all great adventurers need one to help them make the right decisions.

You're going to need a mission control for your money: a place where you can keep track of all your spending and saving, so that you can look back on it and learn about what's working or not working. Right now, your mission control dashboard can be as simple as a couple of pages in a notebook where you write stuff down. As you get older and your money life gets more complicated, you can evolve this into a powerful dashboard. It doesn't matter how simple your first mission control is; what matters is that you start one.[49]

Your money mission control is a place where you need to record what happened in the past, and also plan what you want to do in the future. Your mission control needs to be tracking a couple of things:

1. What do you have or owe (and what's your net worth)?
2. Where did your money go (and what % did you save)?
3. How close are you to your savings goals?

I'm going to give you three options for building a money mission control dashboard. Choose whichever one will be easiest for you.

- **Option 1: Notebook and pen.** Go old-school with a small notebook. I recommend that you get one of those tiny ones that are smaller than your hand, so you can carry it around with you more easily, or even keep it in your wallet if you've got a wallet. This is a great option if you're mostly using cash rather than a bank account.
- **Option 2: A spreadsheet.** If you've got a computer and internet access at home, and if you're comfortable with spreadsheets, I've got a Google Sheets and Excel template for you on the website.
- **Option 3: An app.** If you're lucky enough to have your own smartphone (or if you have very lenient folks who let you borrow theirs a lot) you could install an app. There's a list of recommended apps on the website.

Any of these three options is totally fine!

---

49 If you're a Pokémon fan, think of your first dashboard as being like a Magikarp: it might not look like much, but one day it could turn into a Gyarados, and then you will be UNSTOPPABLE.

Let's go set up your mission control dashboard now, by working through those questions:

What do you have or owe?

Make a list of all the money you already have, or all the money you owe to other people, and what it's worth. That could mean stuff like:

- Bank accounts
- Coins in your piggy bank
- Savings accounts
- That R50 you owe your friend for milkshakes
- Money other friends owe you back
- Gift vouchers stashed in your drawer

If you're using the spreadsheet from the website, it will look like this:

What do I have?	
Account	
Bank account	R159
Savings account	R702
Cash in my piggy bank	R50
Money I owe Kwezi for milkshakes	-R20
Net worth	**R891**

Now, work out your net worth. Remember from Chapter 3 that you calculate your net worth like this:

have – owe = net worth

Right now, that number might be a big fat ZERO. That's okay! We're going to get that number up, trust me.

Where did your money go?

Next, on a new page or in a new part of the spreadsheet, make a list of all your types of income, like allowances, side-hustles and gifts. Put a heading over this that says **MONEY IN**.

Then make a list of the main ways money can leave your life (your main envelopes). Put a heading over this that says **MONEY OUT**. I recommend keeping this simple, so your spreadsheet or list might look something like this:

Category
MONEY IN
Allowance
Side-hustles
Gifts or other money
MONEY OUT
Spent
Saved or invested
Donated to charity

I know that for many of you doing all this homework sounds worse than sprinkling the polio virus over your face, but having a mission control dashboard is the only way to really master your money. Soz.

Now, unlike the support team for actual astronauts, you don't need to be sitting and watching your money dashboard 24/7, peeing into a plastic bag under the table, surviving off bags of chips because you can't peel your eyes away from the screen.[50] In fact, watching your money too closely can be UNHELPFUL, because most of the time you should be making a plan and then just sticking to it. Also, thinking about money all the time makes you a pretty boring person.[51] I want to help you set up such a good system for managing your money that most of the time you don't have to think about it at all.

In fact, I want you to think about your money only **once a week for 10 minutes**, and **once a month for 30 minutes**. That's about one hour a month! That's not so much time! I spend more time than that every month trying to remember where I put my keys.

Every week, you spend 10 minutes doing a **WEEKLY CHECK-IN**.

And then, on the first week of each month, you spend a bit longer making a **MONTHLY ACTION PLAN**.

Your weekly check-in

Here's what you do in your weekly check-in:

1. Check how much money you've got left in each envelope (or bank account).

2. Make sure you know where all your money went in the past week, by checking what you wrote in your note-book, or by checking your transactions on your banking app or online banking website. As you do this, think about each purchase. Was spending this money worth it? Did it bring you more joy or meaning, or did you spend this money because you were feeling sad or awkward or

---

50 At least, this is how I imagine mission control staff live. Hit me up if you know someone who actually works for NASA, who can confirm!

51 Yes, my friends have stopped inviting me to parties.

didn't want to feel left out? The point of doing this isn't to judge yourself, it's just to start to understand your own spending better.

3. Split out the Fun Money you're allowed to spend in the coming week by putting it into a new envelope or moving it into your Fun Money bank account.

Your monthly action plan

Here's what you do in your monthly action plan time.

Step 1: Update your net worth

Write down everything that you have or owe, and check if your net worth has increased since last month.

What do I have?			
Account	Jan 2020	Feb 2020	Mar 2020
Bank account	R203	R226	R196
Savings account	R652	R702	R790
Cash in my piggy bank	R80	R50	R120
Money I owe Kwezi for milkshakes	-R30	-R30	
Net worth	R905	R948	R1 106
Growth since last month		R43	R158

Step 2: Work out where your money went

Write down how much money you spent from each of your envelopes. If you've got any cash left over, move it into savings.

If you're feeling like an extra fundi, work out what percentage of all your money you saved that month. If you're using the spreadsheet, it will do that for you automagically. If you're

Where did my money go?			
Category	**Jan 2020**	**Feb 2020**	**Mar 2020**
Money in	R250	R390	R230
Allowance	R200	R200	R200
Side-hustles	R50	R150	R30
Gifts or other money		R40	
Money out	R250	R390	R230
Spent	R200	R190	R200
Saved or invested	R40	R160	
Donated to charity	R10	R40	R30
What % did I save?	16,00%	41,03%	0,00%

working in a notebook, you'll need to do a little bit of maths here. But only the smallest amount of maths. Just take all the money you saved that month, and divide it by your total income that month. Multiply that by 100. That number is your savings ratio.

> Calculating your savings rate
> savings ÷ income × 100 = savings ratio

This number is your new obsession. Your challenge is to make it as high as humanly possible. Write it on a Post-it and stick it on your bathroom mirror. Tattoo it onto your cat.[52] Think about it as much as you can. And, every month, just try to make it a little bit higher than it was the month before.

---

52 Digby says, 'EXCUSE ME?!'

Step 3: Move your money into the right envelopes

Remember the plan you made earlier, about what percentage of money to put in each of your envelopes? Now's the time to actually move your money to where it should be. You might want to spend a few minutes thinking about the month ahead before you do that: are there any big things you need to buy this month, like a present for your mum's birthday? Some months, you might need to change your plan a little bit. That's fine – being flexible is important.

Go right now and set up a reminder to yourself for your first few WEEKLY REVIEWS, and your first MONTHLY ACTION PLAN time. If you get an allowance monthly, try to do it on the day you receive your allowance. Otherwise, just do it on the first day of each new month.

MAKING YOUR FUN MONEY LAST

Do you find that you're one of those people who ends up spending all of their Fun Money on day 1, and then has nothing left for the rest of the month? Try breaking your Fun Money up into weeks, like this:

- During your Monthly Action Plan, sit down and work out how much money you can safely afford to spend on fun things this month, excluding your savings or other goals. This amount is your Fun Money for the month.
- Divide your Fun Money by four (or five, if it's one of those long months). Transfer a quarter of it into your Fun Money envelope (either a different bank account, or an actual envelope, or money that you draw out as cash).

- Spend your Fun Money. Wheee!
- One week later, transfer another quarter into your Fun Money envelope.
- Repeat.

Here's the beauty of this simple system: you can now just enjoy having fun with that money. You have permission to spend it. In fact, thinking up fun ways to spend it should be your mission! Whatever you spend it on, you don't need to feel guilty about it, because all of your Responsible Savings Money or Charity Money is safely tucked away in a different envelope.

There is only one very important rule that makes this system work: when you are out of Fun Money, you are out of Fun Money. If this means you can't afford to buy a cooldrink when all your friends are getting one so you have to sit there drinking tap water, then so be it. You'll never be broke for more than seven days at a time with this system, so just suck it up.

Phew! That chapter was a lot of work, but you did it. Here's a picture of a balloon cat to say congratulations. You've EARNED it.

IN SUMMARY!

- Put your money into envelopes that protect you from ever spending more than you want to. These envelopes can be real paper envelopes for cash, or they can be different bank accounts. You also need a plan for how you'll split your money between your envelopes.
- You can't manage what you don't measure, so you need a money mission control dashboard.
- Every week, spend 10 minutes thinking about where your money went in the past week, and check how much is left in your envelopes.
- Every month, update your dashboard and put your plan into action.

Chapter 9

GROW THAT DOUGH

BE NICE TO FUTURE YOU

Remember a long, long time ago, all the way back in Chapter 3, where we learnt about **compound interest** and how the longer you leave money, the bigger it grows? This chapter is all about how to grow that money.

Compound interest is what makes saving MAGICAL. If you can hold out on spending all of your money now, and instead save some of it, you'll have way more money at the end of the day.

Normally, when you think about saving, you think about saving FOR specific things. You might hear your friends say, 'I'm saving up *for* that new video game about flying sharks,' or 'I'm saving up *for* light-up sneakers that play music announcing when you walk into a room.' That kind of saving is really fun, and important! But it's not the only kind of saving you should do.

Your life has a fog of war, right? Do you ever play strategy-based computer games where you can only see a portion of the map around you, and everything else is hidden behind a fog of war, until you actually go there and see what's there?

Your life is the same. You are far surer about things you want now, and next week, and this year, than you are about things that you might want in five or ten years' time. That means you over-value the things you know about right now.

But money works in exactly the opposite way to how our brains work. Future money is much more valuable than present money, if you've invested it. So, I don't think you should design your savings strategy just around goals. I think you should design your strategy around how money works, and build up a nice big pile of possibility money – your Freedom Fund – and then do whatever you like with it. Especially when you're young.

It's nice to have SOME special things you're saving up for, because it's a great way to motivate you to side-hustle. Why don't you spend a few minutes thinking about some things you'd like to buy? Make sure that you list them in order of priority, with the most important things at the top. If you're using the mission control spreadsheet, there's a tab there for you to keep track of those things (and which tells you if you've got enough saved). It looks like this:

Savings wish list		
How much do I have saved?		200
Goal	What does it cost?	Can I afford it?
Flowers for Mum	R50	Yup!
Video game about flying sharks	R200	Not yet
New sneakers	R500	Not yet
A car when I'm 18	R30 000	Not yet

START WITH A SAVINGS ACCOUNT

The best place to start growing your money is with a simple savings account. This is a bank account that pays you interest.[53] It's a great way to stash money if you don't want to spend it NOW, but that you'll probably want to spend soon (in the next year or so). It's also a great place to temporarily store money that you plan to invest later.

With savings accounts, you usually get a higher interest rate the more you have saved. For example, here's the interest you can earn from Capitec (at the time I was writing this):

Amount saved	Interest rate
R0 – R24 999	4,5%
R25 000 – R99 000	4,75%
R100 000 +	5,25%

You can also get more interest if you're happy to give the bank some warning before you take your money out (often 7 days, or 32 days). But usually you have to have a lot of money saved before you can access these types of accounts (often R20 000 and over).

Get the best savings account your existing bank offers. You're not going to earn enough interest on it to make it worth shopping around too much when you're starting out. The interest rates between the banks on these types of accounts don't vary too much.

If your savings have built up to a humongous amount (like over R100 000), though, then you should do some research into something called a money market account (and you should REALLY be investing some of that money).

---

53 Remember from Chapter 3 that interest is money the bank is paying you because you're lending them money.

The rule of 72

The rule of 72 is a nifty little bit of maths that lets you work out how soon you will double your money, if you are saving at a particular interest rate.

$$72 \div \text{ the interest rate } = \text{ number of years to double your money}$$

For example, if you're saving R1 000 in an account that earns 6% interest a year, it will take you $72 \div 6 = 12$ years for your savings to double to R2 000.

Pay your future self first

Savings is the most important envelope you have, so when you're doing your Monthly Action Plan, it should always be the first money you put away.

Normally, when we think about how we want to save more, we think like this: *I'm going to be SUPER-GOOD and stop getting treats from the tuck shop and basically never buy things and then at the end of the month I'm going to have a nice big wad of cash I can stuff into that savings account! Yeah! LOOK AT ME GO.* And then the month actually happens and there's a cute pair of sneakers on sale and a person has to eat more than sandwiches and all your friends are going to the movies tonight and you don't want to be a social pariah and you forgot it's your brother's birthday and what are you a monster you have to buy him a present and then and then and then …

And then the month is over and you've spent everything in your bank account. And that doesn't mean you have no self-control or are a terrible person. It just means you're a normal human being, with the brain of a primate.

So, give your little primate brain some help, and flip the narrative around:

'You don't save what's left after spending. You spend what's left after saving.' Warren Buffett said that (remember him? Fourth richest person in the world?). Warren Buffett's a pretty smart dude.

MEET INFLATION: THE ENEMY OF SAVING

Saving is awesome: it's like a magic elf sitting quietly on your hoard of money making it grow though compound interest. There's just one problem, though: saving has a nemesis that undoes all of its hard work – something called **inflation**.

When I was your age, a can of Coke used to cost R2 at my school tuck shop. Now it costs R9 or more. It's not like the cans of Coke got bigger or more delicious. They're the same as they always were. They cost more because my R1 now is worth less than it was worth 20 years ago. That's inflation.

Inflation happens for a few different reasons: if the cost of manufacturing things increases (like if the oil price goes up), if the number of consumers increases faster than how efficiently we produce things, or if the government puts more money into the economy by printing it or taking on national debt. Some countries have higher levels of inflation than others. South Africa's inflation averages about 6% a year (but it can go much higher or lower than that), while America's is more like 2%. If you use the rule of 72 (try it), you'll see that prices for stuff in South Africa double every 12 years, and prices in America double every 36 years. That extra 4% of inflation makes a big difference.

Now, here's the problem: let's say that you really want to

buy that flying-shark game. So you put your money in a savings account, and you save and you save for a whole year. If you had money in a Capitec savings account, it would have grown at 4.5%. But a year later, your game is now 6% more expensive! That means that your savings won't grow fast enough to keep up with inflation![54]

Ironically, the most dangerous place to store your money is in cash, under your mattress: not because of kleptomaniac tokoloshes, but because inflation means its value decreases every day. If you store it in a savings account, it will grow slowly, but possibly not as much as you need it to. That's why you can't just keep your money in a savings account for too long: you've got to invest it, to try to grow it faster than inflation can eat it away.

As a simple rule of thumb, if you're saving for something that's more than one year away, you should invest that money instead.

Inflation gone MAD

The government is always fiddling to try to keep inflation low while still helping the economy grow. Sometimes they get this wrong, and inflation gets out of control. This is called hyperinflation, and it destroys economies.

In Hungary in 1946, prices were doubling every 15 hours. Imagine if a cool drink cost R10 today, R1 280 in five days' time, and R1 407 374 883 553 280 by the end of the month!

---

54 There will be times when the interest rate you can get on savings accounts will be higher than the inflation rate, so this isn't always true, but it often is.

UNDERSTANDING ASSETS

If you remember from Chapter 3, **investing** means **buying assets**. Assets are things that earn money for you, or increase in value over time. An asset is like a little side-hustle that goes out and side-hustles FOR you, while you get to laze about playing Xbox/singing to your snorgles/having tea with your folks.

Let's pretend, for the lulz, that you went out and bought yourself a wheelbarrow worth R500. What could you do with it?

Well, you could just toodle around and have fun with it. You could line it with plastic sheeting and fill it with water and call it a tiny Jacuzzi. You could challenge other kids with wheelbarrows to races around the parking lot at your school. A wheelbarrow you're using this way isn't an asset, because it's not making you any money – it's just helping you live your life. After a few years of using it, if you tried to sell your wheelbarrow, you'd get much less money than you bought it for.

Or you could use that wheelbarrow to start a little side-hustle, meeting people outside the local shop and offering to cart their heavy groceries home for them. Same wheelbarrow, but now it's a working asset, and it's actually making you dough. Nice! That money you spent on a wheelbarrow was now an investment. It's an investment because you took some money that you had and you put it into an asset in the hopes of growing that money into more money.

Now let's say that you wanted the wheelbarrow to make you money, but you don't actually want to spend all day doing the hard work of wheeling groceries around. But your neighbour already runs a little grocery-wheeling business, and she's much better at making money from this game than you are. She's already got regular customers, and she's hired other kids to wheel groceries around, and she knows all the cheap places to get the wheelbarrows fixed if they break. So, rather than going out and buying the wheelbarrow yourself, you could just give your neighbour the R500 cash, in exchange for a piece of her business and her profits.

Congratulations: you just invented the stock market.

Now, buying **shares** is basically this last wheelbarrow deal. You buy a piece of an existing business. The business uses that cash to grow, and you get a share of the profits (they're called 'dividends'). And your ownership of that tiny bit of the company is an asset in its own right: you can sell your piece of the business to someone else.

Shares are sometimes called stocks or equities. Usually, people mean more or less the same thing when they use these different terms.

Lots of countries have stock markets, and shares in all of the big companies you've heard of are bought and sold through them. South Africa's stock market is called the Johannesburg Stock Exchange (JSE for short), and you can buy pieces of companies like MTN and Mr Price and Steers. You can also buy shares in international companies through the global stock markets, where you'll find companies like BMW, Apple, Nike, Netflix or Disney. Shares in almost all the big companies in the world are for sale. If you've heard of it, you can probably buy a piece of it.

Think of a stock market as being like a mall where you can buy businesses. Stock markets used to be real-world marketplaces where people would stand around and buy and sell bits of companies to each other in person, but now they're all online. You can buy shares through apps or websites just like you can buy jeans or video games.

But back to our wheelbarrow for a second. Let's say you don't want to buy a piece of your neighbour's wheelbarrow business, but you still want to invest your R500. You could make a deal with your neighbour in which you loan her the money so that she can buy a new wheelbarrow for her business, and she promises to pay you back R550 in a year's time. That's called a bond. Shares mean owning a piece of a business; bonds mean lending money to a business. Boom! Now you know some finance words.

Underneath all this finance voodoo you hear about – shares, bonds, the financial economy – there's the real economy. Finance people don't really make money grow using magic fairy dust (although they'd like you to think they do). Your money grows when companies in the real world use that money in their businesses.

Most people are poep-scared of the idea of investing. They think it's like gambling, or it's something only rich people do. But guess what? You can start investing with as little as R10, and it doesn't take a long time to learn. And if you understand what you're doing, it doesn't have to be very risky. With new websites popping up all the time that make buying shares super-easy, it's also really quick to do.

Isn't that cool? Like, I'm obsessed with the Steers Wacky Wednesday 2-for-1 burger special. I buy it once a month, and it costs me R60 each time. Instead of buying that R60 burger, I could buy R60 worth of Steers the company instead,[55] and it would literally take as much time as standing in line to order the burger.

---

55 Technically, you'd buy shares in Famous Brands, the company that owns Steers.

Weird assets

In my opinion, investing through the stock market is the best way to start investing. The stock market's great, because it's easy, you can start with very little money, and it can be relatively safe if you do it properly. But there are a whole bunch of other types of assets you might explore over your lifetime:

- Owning direct shares in a business (not through the stock market), often because it's a business that you started.
- Buying property. There are a lot of different ways to do this: one of my favourites is to buy shares in a company that owns a lot of properties (this is called a real estate investment trust or REIT). You could also buy properties to rent to other people, which gives you an income, or buy properties that you hope will be worth more when you sell them.
- Buying precious metals like LITERAL BARS OF GOLD. Yup, people actually do this.
- Buying foreign currency, like dollars or yen, and hoping that its value will increase more in relation to rands over time.
- Buying Bitcoin, Ethereum and other forms of digital assets or cryptocurrencies.
- Buying art, rare sneakers, old cars or other collectibles. My friend Georgina likes to call this 'the lunatic fringe of investing', because it's really hard to make money doing this unless you really know what you're doing.
- Buying cows. This is a very important form of investment in many traditional communities in South Africa, but now you can also buy a cow through an app (it's called Livestock Wealth) and someone else will look

after it for you. There are also new apps that let you buy stuff like blueberry bushes or bees. Isn't the future weird?

All of these types of assets are interesting, but don't worry about them for now. The stock market is the best type of investment to learn first. Once you've got that figured out, it can be fun to start exploring weirder assets.

Be aware that there are many things that are marketed as 'investment opportunities' that are really just scams (popular ones at the moment talk about trading 'forex' or crypto-currencies). Do your research before you give anyone your money, and don't believe anyone who promises you better returns than the long-term historical stock market average (7% above inflation a year).

WOBBLY INVESTMENTS

When you own shares, their value goes up and down all the time. One minute a share could be worth R100, and the next minute it might be worth R12 or R305 or nothing. The price wobbles around all over the place, because a share is worth whatever the last person who bought the share was prepared to pay for it. That could have been influenced by all sorts of things: recent news about that company, the politics of the country that business is registered in, even what the weather was like on that day (no, really).

This price wobbliness can feel really weird and scary! But it's just how the stock market works. Over the long run, the prices will ultimately wobble up. They've been doing that for over 100 years. In fact, the wobbliness of shares is part of WHY they end up higher in the long run.

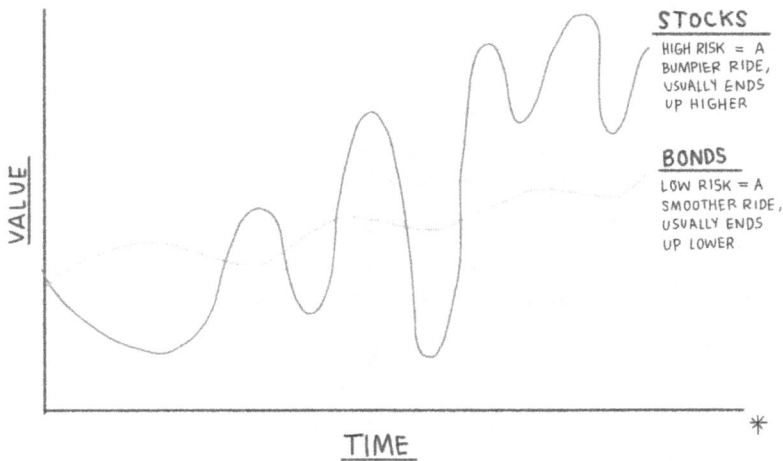

STOCKS
HIGH RISK = A BUMPIER RIDE, USUALLY ENDS UP HIGHER

BONDS
LOW RISK = A SMOOTHER RIDE, USUALLY ENDS UP LOWER

VALUE

TIME

✳ THIS IS PURELY ILLUSTRATIVE & NOT A REAL GRAPH

This means that shares are a LONG-TERM investment, not a way to get rich quick. There are some people who try to make money by timing the wobbles and buying and selling shares quickly (often, many times in the same day). I call that **speculation**, not investing, and most people lose money trying to speculate. Investing means buying into the long-term growth of an asset and its profits. It's playing the long game.

People lose money in the stock market when they try to make money quickly. Let me show you how that works.

Imagine you want to buy shares in a business called Fake Dog Poo Incorporated, which sells gag gifts. You buy your first share, which costs R100.

And hey, a month later, your one share of Fake Dog Poo Incorporated is now worth R130! WOOHOO! You've already made a profit. You realise this is clearly a great investment, so you decide to buy four more shares. Now, you've invested R620. But in month three, the shares aren't doing as well, and now your shares have actually gone down a bit in price and are worth R120 each. You still think it's a good investment, though, so you buy one more share. Now you've invested R740 and you own six shares.

And then disaster strikes: an article comes out in the newspaper alleging that one of the ingredients in Fake Dog Poo Incorporated's fake dog poo product is . . . real dog poo! The price of the shares drops down to R50 overnight, and now your six shares that cost you R740 are worth only R300. You get a fright and sell all your shares, having lost R440. Ouch.

And then, to add insult to injury, it turns out that the article was a hoax and the share price goes back up over the next two months. Except, you don't own any shares any more, so this doesn't help you.

If you try to time the market

	Month 1	Month 2	Month 3	Month 4	Month 5	Month 6
Price of one stock	R100	R130	R120	R50	R90	R110
How many shares you own	1	5	6	6	0	0
Amount you've invested	R100	R620	R740	R740	R740	R740
What your shares are worth	R100	R650	R720	R300	R0	R0
Profit on your shares	R0	R30	-R20	-4R40	-R440	-R440

This is what happens when most people try to time the stock market: they end up buying when the shares are at their most expensive, and selling when their shares are at their cheapest. It's just human nature.

Now, here's what would have happened if you completely ignored what the share price was doing, and you just bought one share every month, no matter where the share price was wobbling to:

If you just invest the same amount every month						
	Month 1	Month 2	Month 3	Month 4	Month 5	Month 6
Price of one shares	R100	R130	R120	R50	R90	R110
How many shares you own	1	2	3	4	5	6
Amount you've invested	R100	R230	R350	R400	R490	R600
What your shares are worth	R100	R260	R360	R200	R450	R660
Profit on your shares	R0	R30	R10	-R200	-R40	R60

You'd have bought some shares when they were cheap, and some shares when they were expensive. And overall, you would have made a perfectly respectable profit of R60, enough to buy plenty of fake dog poo to slip into your sibling's school bag.

Investing is one of those areas of your life where laziness is your best friend. Just try to buy the same amount every month and don't worry about timing the market.

There will be some times when the WHOLE stock market will crash, and all of the shares you own will lose a lot of their value very quickly. This happens every few years, and it can be frightening! But it helps to remember that it's just a temporary wobble. The worst year the American stock market ever had was 1931, when it lost 43% in one year. But the funny thing is, just two years later, 1933, was the *best* year the American stock market ever had, when it gained 54%.

Performance of the 500 biggest companies in America

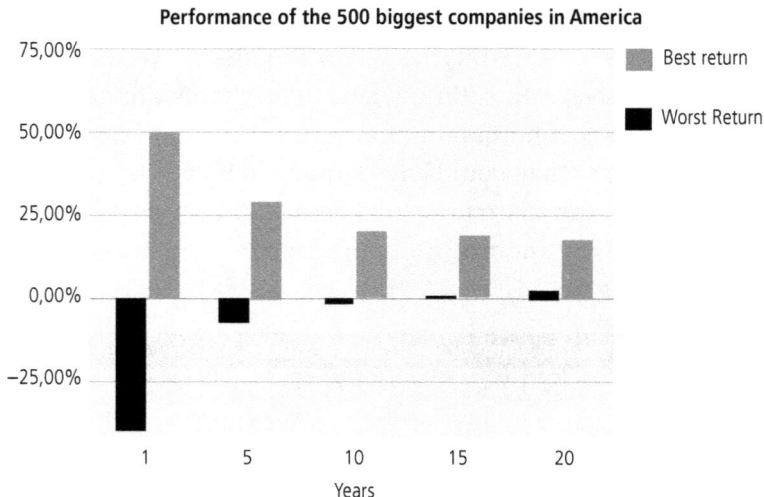

The thing to do when the stock market crashes is *nothing* – just wait. The market will wobble the other way soon, and your shares will eventually be worth more than they were when you started. That 'eventually' might be one year, or it might be ten. That's why you shouldn't put all your money in the stock market if you know that you want to spend it within the next five years.

- If you want money in less than a year from now, keep it in a cash savings account.
- If you want money between one year and five years from now, keep some of it in bonds and some of it in shares.
- If you want money in more than five years, keep it in shares.

It's definitely possible to lose money investing in the stock market! But it becomes less and less likely, the longer you invest for. And NOT investing over the long run is even riskier, because inflation is just going to eat all your savings away.

Remember that shares are a high-risk, high-reward asset. The more time you have to invest, the higher the risk you should be taking. You're young, which means that you've got LOTS of time on your side. Over the last 100 years, no other type of asset has grown as well as shares. Not property, not gold, not art, not rare *Magic: The Gathering* cards, nothing. Buying bits of companies might feel like this weird, intangible thing, but in the long run, it's the thing that's most reliably going to keep your money safe from inflation, and make it easier than you think to afford your biggest dreams.

So go ahead, young friend, and wobble that money.

How much can I expect to earn if I invest in shares?

It's impossible to say for sure how much money you'll earn from investing in shares, but you can guess that it will probably be somewhere around the long-term average. These have been the average amounts over the past 100 years or so:[56]

	Shares	**Bonds**
South Africa	7% above inflation	1% above inflation
World	5% above inflation	2% above inflation

Notice that these are returns ABOVE inflation, which are also called **real returns.** So, if inflation was 6% and the real return was 7%, the overall growth would have been about 13% (which, if you remember the rule of 72, means your money would double every six years).

---

56   Source: Credit Suisse Global Investment Returns Tables 2019.

That's a lot better than the 4–5% the bank will give you in a savings account.

Remember, in some years shares will grow much less than this (or lose you money) and in some years they will grow more than this. The average just gives you an idea of what to expect.

The real power of shares happens when you leave them alone for a long time, and let compound interest do its special magic. At 13% growth, every R1 000 you invest when you're 10 will turn into R13 000 when you're 30.

THE SMARTER, SAFER WAY TO INVEST

Okay, but here's the flaw with this whole plan. Let's say that you want to buy shares, but you have no idea which share you should buy. You don't want to have to spend your whole life becoming an expert in share picking! Some people get a real kick out of this stuff, but most of us find it pretty boring.

Well, it turns out that this is one of the few places in life where doing the easiest thing is actually the smartest thing for most people.

You see, there are two ways to invest in shares. The one way is to pick individual companies to invest in. Say you want to buy shares in a fast-food company. You could do a bunch of research and try to figure out who is making better burgers: Steers or Burger King. This will require eating a LOT of burgers, just to be sure.[57] So, you figure out who's making the best burger, and who's got the best business, and you bet everything on that company over all the others.

---

57 I volunteer! I volunteer!

But doing that kind of research takes a lot of time. And a person can only eat so many burgers. So they normally give their money to a professional share picker who does this for them. This is what you're doing when you go to a fancy dude in an Audi who works for one of the investment companies and puts it in one of their funds. It's called **active investing**, because you're actively trying to find the winning shares (or you're trying to find the winning share picker).

The other way to buy shares is what's called passive investing. Instead of figuring out whether Burger King is better than Steers, you just buy both of them. In fact, you buy every single company you can. Usually, you do this through something called an **index tracker fund**.

You might have heard of the Top 40? That's the 40 biggest companies in South Africa. Or the S&P 500? That's the 500 biggest companies in America. You can even buy index funds that track the whole world in one product, like the Vanguard Total World Stock Index Fund, the Ashburton Global 1200 or the Satrix MSCI World Fund.[58]

If you invest in one of those things, you're putting your money into companies in Rwanda, in Australia, in Japan, everywhere. You're literally investing in all the businesses of the world in one go. That means that these are extremely safe investments, because the chances of all of these businesses failing at the same time are very low, unless there's a meteor or something, in which case you've got bigger problems to worry about.

And here's the other great thing about investing like that:

---

58   A lot of funds like this are called ETFs, which stands for 'exchange-traded funds'. Sorry, finance people like to give things strange names.

buying index funds is super-cheap. You're not buying an Audi for some fancy share picker. And the data shows that 80% of the time, the passive funds BEAT the active funds. That's right: doing the easy thing is probably going to make you more money than doing the hard thing. AND it's going to be much safer, because you're not putting all your eggs in one basket. Sweet!

When you're starting out, I strongly suggest that your first investment is a simple index tracker fund, ideally one that covers the whole world and not just South Africa.

Investment fees matter more than you think

When you're looking to buy your first investment, take a look at the fees the investment company wants to charge you for buying the shares or index fund. These fees look really small: they're usually between 1% and 4% of whatever your investment is worth, every year.

The problem is that the **real growth** on your investments is probably only 7% a year, which means that a fee of 4% will eat up more than HALF of the growth of your investments!

Fees compound, just like investment growth does. So they matter much more than you think. It's worth shopping around to find fees of 1% or lower when you're investing in an index fund. The investment company often calls their fees EAC (Effective Annual Cost) or TER (Total Expense Ratio). This is just another way that investment companies try to baffle you with nonsense so you get confused and feel like you need to buy a fancy share picker an Audi to do it for you, but persevere! I believe in you!

How much an investment of R100 000 is worth after 40 years

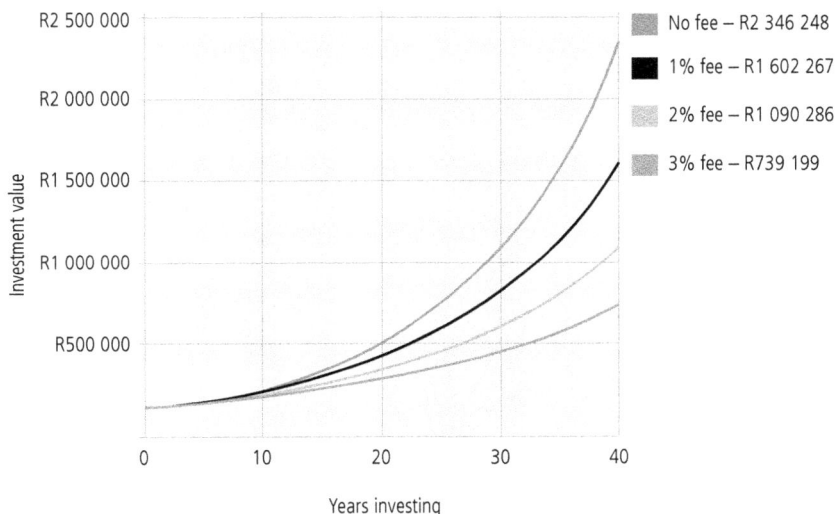

Free money, aka the tax-free savings account

Friends, I have something exciting to tell you: the government wants to give you free money!

Normally, when you make money from investing, the government wants a cut of your profits. This is called tax – we'll talk about it more in Chapter 11.

But the government also wants to encourage you to invest your money (it's good for the economy if you do), so you're allowed to invest a chunk of money every year into something called a TFSA (tax-free savings account). You don't have to pay taxes on any of the profits in your TFSA, ever, no matter how big it gets. You're allowed to open a TFSA from the day you're born.

A TFSA is like an invisibility cloak: you can put almost any kind of investment underneath it and it will become invisible to the taxman. You can wrap your TFSA around an index fund, or even a regular savings account at the bank.

The TFSA has limits, though. Each person is allowed to invest R33 000 a year into it, up to a maximum of R550 000 over their lifetime. Once you've used up a chunk of that allowance, it's gone forever, so you don't want to use your TFSA for savings that you're going to take out again within the next couple of years. Save your TFSA wrapper for really long-term, high-growth investments like shares rather than cash savings. If you're building up a Freedom Fund for yourself, the TFSA is a great place for it.

Beware of bubbles and fads

In the 1600s, tulips were introduced to Amsterdam. The Dutch had never seen such gorgeous flowers, and having tulips growing in your garden became a status symbol. Tulips were the R1 000 Nike shoes of their day.

So the price of tulip bulbs started to rise. No problem, right? Lots of people want to buy something so its price goes up. Except that, suddenly, a bunch of businesspeople noticed that the price was rising, and they started speculating: buying contracts for future tulips, hoping that the price would continue to rise and they could sell them at a profit. This pushed the prices up even higher, which led to more speculation, which pushed the prices higher still. It was tulip mania.

Prices went crazy. Soon it got so bad that tulip traders started selling everything they owned to invest in a couple of tulip bulbs. Tulips were being bought and sold on the stock exchange. It reached the point where one tulip bulb cost about ten times the annual income of a regular Dutch worker.

The problem was, the people buying and selling tulips didn't actually want tulips, they were just hoping that the price would keep rising.

This, my friends, is called a bubble. And, at some point, all bubbles pop.

Eventually, the mood changed on tulips, and people started panicking. Everyone started trying to sell their tulip contracts at the same time, but suddenly no one wanted to buy them. People had poured all of their money into an asset that was now worth almost zero. As a result, the whole country's economy went into a depression that lasted for years.

Bubbles will happen in your lifetime. If everyone's talking about how you can make fast money by investing in some trendy, high-growth asset, block your ears. If it sounds too good to be true, it probably is.

Be a lazy investor

One of the big investment companies in America, Fidelity, once did this in-depth study about which of its investors had the best-performing portfolios over the long term. It turns out that the ones who made the best investments were the people who'd actually forgotten they had an account.[59]

I know that sounds nuts! But investing rewards people who are patient, and who find an investing strategy and just stick to it, because those are people who aren't reacting emotionally when the market does its normal wobbles.

When you have more experience in investing, you might want to get more involved in picking good assets. But when you're starting out, just find one really broad, cheap index fund that covers as much of the world as possible, and invest into it every month, the same amount, regardless of what the market is doing. If you've got a bank account, a great

---

59 http://www.businessinsider.com/forgetful-investors-performed-best-2014-9 is where you'll find the full story.

way to do this is to set up a recurring payment that goes off your account automatically.

The fancy term for this is 'rand cost averaging'. I call it 'being smart and lazy'. Doing this, you'll end up buying shares when they're 'on sale' and end up with much more overall. Just focus on putting as much into your investment as you can, every month, and leave it there to do its magic for a decade or two. And try not to peek.

Enough theory! The best way to learn how to invest is to actually go and practise investing. You don't need to do this with real money, to begin with: start by opening up a virtual portfolio, where you invest fake money into real shares, and see how much money you would have made.

Go online now and find a website that lets you create a virtual portfolio. There are some suggestions on the website. Buy an easy, low-cost index fund with your fake money. Leave it for a while and watch it wobble!

Once you're feeling comfortable investing fake money, start investing for realzies. Start with a tiny amount, like R10. You'll need a real bank account for this, and I suggest you get your folks to help you. I bet you'll love seeing all that money rolling in, that you didn't even have to go out and earn.

IN SUMMARY!

- Savings accounts are great for money you want to spend within the next year.
- Inflation is the enemy of saving. Investing your money is the best way to help it grow faster than inflation.

- The stock market isn't as mysterious as it sounds: it just means buying pieces of successful companies. It's the best-performing type of asset over the long term, but it's very wobbly in the short term.
- The best way to invest safely is to bet on LOTS of things rather than a few things. An easy, low-cost way to do this is by investing in an index fund.
- You're likely to lose money trying to time the market, pick shares or follow fads – unless you REALLY know what you're doing. Being lazy and investing the same amount of money every month into a simple index fund is a great way to start.

Chapter 10

RESIST MIND CONTROL (AKA ADVERTISING)

I'm going to sound like a crazy conspiracy nut for a minute, but I want to let you in on something. There are people out there who are trying to hijack your brain and control your thoughts. I'm not talking about alien invaders or super-villains: I'm talking about advertisers.

Every business in the world wants you to buy the things they're selling. That's not a bad thing by itself, but it does mean that they spend billions and billions of rands each year on marketing and advertising, industries whose sole aim is to make you think you want a bunch of stuff you didn't want before they told you that you want it. These people are crazy-good at their jobs. They shape a lot of the ideas you find in the culture around you; they make people believe things like 'cars mean freedom' and 'no one will love you unless you are a very specific type of beautiful' and 'expensive means quality'. But these ideas are not your own. They have been carefully implanted in your brain so that you buy things. They distract you from the things you really do care about.

The way to resist mind control is to understand your own mind. Remember: your brain is a lot more like the brain of a monkey than like a computer. It's got specific weaknesses, and advertisers are very good at using those weaknesses to get us to buy things. When you spend money, you think it's because you rationally decided to buy something.

But often, you just spend money because you are being manipulated.

Outsmart the advertisers by knowing your brain's own weaknesses![60] I'll even teach you the technical names for these brain quirks, in brackets, so you can impress people at parties.

Sounds about right (anchoring)

You have no internal, preset idea of what most things should cost, so the first number that you happen to hear is normally the one that will set your idea of normal. Think about it like this: If you go into a shop where all the T-shirts are priced between R320 and R550, spending R400 on one doesn't seem too bad. But if you walk around the corner into a different shop, where they start at R60 and end at R120, suddenly R400 seems like a ridiculous amount to spend.

Sometimes, restaurants even put a particularly expensive item on the menu that they don't expect anyone ever to buy – it's just there to make everything else seem reasonable by comparison.

The way to beat anchoring is to shop around before you buy something big, so you can get a proper idea of what something really should cost.

FOMO (scarcity)

You're much more likely to buy something if you feel rushed to make a decision. Businesses use this trick all the time by putting fake time pressure on things.

---

60 I have a secret to confess: I worked in advertising for a lot of my 20s, so I know how this stuff works. People who work in advertising aren't bad people, really. It's the whole system of consumer capitalism that's broken, that needs people to be buying stuff all the time to keep making billionaires richer.

One way they do this is by calling something a 'limited edition' or by making it seem like there's only one left of something (often, they'll hide more of the same product in a back room) so you think you've got to buy it NOW before it runs out (and you don't have time to think about it).

Another way businesses make you feel rushed is by having sales. Buying something that you *already wanted* when it's actually on sale is a great idea. But how often have you been duped into buying something only *because* it's on sale? No judgement, buddy, I've been bamboozled by this one many times.

What's even worse is that sometimes businesses just flat-out lie about something being on sale. Sure, it says it's 50% cheaper than normal, but how can you be sure unless you checked what the price was before the sale? Companies have even been caught putting their prices UP in the month before Black Friday (the biggest con there is), just so they can say that the Black Friday discount is bigger than it really is.

How you resist this form of mind control is by keeping a wish list of the big stuff you want to buy, and keeping track of what its price is (there's space for you to do this if you're using the spreadsheet for your money mission control dashboard). That way, you can tell if that so-called sale price really is as good as it looks. And remember that if you're feeling rushed to buy something, you're probably being manipulated.

Falling for cuteness (anthropomorphism)

Here's a wonderful thing about our brains: we're programmed to want to love and look after helpless baby creatures. That's why we're all suckers for videos of baby otters, or tiny goats in pyjamas, or snuggly piglets cuddling teddy bears.[61] We are powerless against the forces of cuteness!

Businesses know this, and they invest a bunch of time and money in making their products look cuter or more human so that we unconsciously bond with them.

Once you pop . . . (choice momentum)

Once you say yes to something, you're more likely to say yes to something else. Salespeople sometimes use this trick by first asking you a question that they know you'll agree to (like, 'Do you love your cat?') which makes you more likely to say yes to the next question ('Well then I'm sure you'll be interested in buying this diamond-encrusted cat bed, right?').

This is also why, once you've decided to buy ONE thing in a shop, it feels much easier to buy five more things (which is why there are sweets lined up by the till in supermarkets).

Distraction (the decoy effect)

Businesses will try to distract you by making you focus on comparing the features of two different options, and make you forget that you also need to compare that purchase against *everything else you could be doing with that money.*

Let's say you see two backpacks for sale, one for R200 and one for R250. You get so caught up trying to decide whether the glow-in-the-dark stitching on backpack #2 is worth the extra R50 that you forget that you should also be asking whether you would rather be spending that money on something that isn't a backpack! That's also called the opportunity cost: the new backpack is also *costing* you, say, 20 soft drinks you could have had instead of the backpack.

---

61   I'm squealing just writing this.

Jumping on the bandwagon (herd mentality)

All of us want to fit in. All of us want to be loved and accepted. That's totally normal! What's not normal is how marketers have manipulated society so that being accepted means buying the right brands.

Branding is a major way that advertisers try to make money out of your need to be accepted by your peers. You can see this by looking at the branding on clothes and equipment in the main teen subcultures, where often a huge part of it is getting to hang out with your group while doing the thing you love – like surfing, skateboarding, tech, gaming, sports, listening to certain kinds of music. Advertisers want you to believe that you can just buy your way into these groups by wearing the clothes or buying the brands they're associated with. But really, if you want to be a surfer, the best way is to actually learn to surf!

When I was thirteen, every girl in my school wanted these really chunky shoes called Buffalos. All the cool girls had them. Boy oh boy, did I want a pair of those shoes.[62] There was just one problem: I was on a scholarship at a private school, so all my friends came from families that had a lot more money than mine did. My parents were already working multiple jobs and side-hustles to support our family (the humans and the animals), and there definitely wasn't any spare money for brand-name clothes. My sweet mum went out and bought me a pair of shoes that *looked* like Buffalos, but they were a knock-off brand (probably called Puffalos or something). I was mortified, and remember trying to explain to her that wearing fakes would be worse than going to school barefoot. Because the whole point of the shoes wasn't what

---

62   Come to think of it, I STILL want them.

they looked like or how they felt – it was the brand name. The brand name was what made them cool.

Isn't that nuts? That's how well marketers were mind-controlling me. They were mind-controlling my whole school.

In the end, I never got my Buffalos. About six months later, they went out of fashion and everyone stopped wearing them.

You'll see a lot of fads in your lifetime. It's worth remembering that they all pass. And also that most people don't actually care about what you're wearing – they're too busy worried that people are judging THEM to even have space in their brains for judging you! And as you get older, you'll see that the really cool people were the ones who were learning how to make their own style rather than just buying into trends.

Influencers (social norming)

Marketers don't just use your real friends to influence you into thinking you need to buy their stuff. They also use fake friends!

I really love the way that social media lets you have a personal connection with people you'll never meet in real life. I spend a lot of time on YouTube and TikTok and Instagram, and I follow a lot of influencers who sometimes feel like real friends to me. I'm really glad that people put so much time and effort into making content that teaches me stuff, makes me laugh and makes me feel less alone in the world.

But never forget that influencers also get paid money to promote certain products and shape our perception about what's desirable.

Marketers even pay to put their products in the movies and TV shows we watch, and sometimes even make shows or movies as advertisements in disguise (for example, the TV show *Transformers* was invented by a toy company called Hasbro to sell toys to kids).

Here's something to remember when you're feeling jealous of the lives of others: what you see on social media are just the BEST parts of someone else's life. You're seeing

♥ 224 LIKES
COOLBB #travel #friends

the photos where they look especially cool, the most fun adventures they go on, the best times they had out with their friends. You're not seeing the fact that, most of the time, they're just as awkward, bored and lonely as you sometimes feel.

Targeted ads (personalisation)

Whenever you do something online, advertisers use it to build up a profile of who you are, and they use it to tailor ads especially to you, so you're more likely to buy something.

Want to see something creepy? If you have a device that you regularly use Google on, go to this link, and take a look at all the stuff Google knows about you: https://myaccount. google.com/data-and-personalization

Involving your senses (Pavlovian responses)

The music, artwork, colours and everything else about advertisements have been carefully worked out to appeal to you. The style and aesthetic are a huge part of advertising – and a lot of it can actually be pretty cool. But did you know that marketers use music, colour, smell and touch in shops to attract shoppers too?

Music can change your mood by affecting your heartbeat and triggering a chemical called dopamine that makes you feel good. Classical music can increase the sense that something has value, while slow music slows you down and increases the time and money you spend in a store.

Some supermarkets pump the smell of freshly baked goods into the air to get shoppers to feel homely and relaxed. Floral scents are known to make shoppers browse longer and spend more. A study by an American neurologist called Dr Alan Hirsch showed that 84% of people would pay $10 more for a pair of Nike shoes if the room had a nice smell pumped into it!

It turns out that we're not that different from Pavlov's dog, the one who started expecting food whenever he heard a bell ring. Marketers can train us so that we start to associate certain purchases with other triggers, like how you start thinking about popcorn as soon as you go to the movies, or why jingles that get stuck in your head are so powerful.

Sounds like manipulation, doesn't it? But you can fight back!

STRATEGIES FOR SAVVY SPENDING
Delete advertising from your life

Advertising exists to make you think you need stuff that you did not need until you saw the ad. Ads are never going to bring you anything but misery and poverty. Cut them out of your life.

If you use a digital device, install an ad blocker that hides ads from you. If you watch old-school TV, get into the habit of turning the sound off when ads come on.

Malls are advertisements you walk through, so stay out of them. Never buy magazines: they're literally huge piles of glossy ads that make you pay money for the pleasure of being advertised to. If you are becoming a shopaholic, you should even consider deleting your Instagram account – it's just a fancier collection of magazine ads that never ends.

This cool graffiti artist I like, called Banksy, said this about advertising:

[Advertisers] butt into your life, take a cheap shot at you and then disappear. They leer at you from tall buildings and make you feel small. They make flippant comments from buses that imply you're not sexy enough and that all the fun is happening somewhere else. They are on TV making [you] feel inadequate. They have access to the most sophisticated technology the world has ever seen and they bully you with it.

Don't put up with bullies. Clear as much advertising out of your life as you can.

Learn to say no to your friends

I have learnt from painful experience not to go shopping with my friend Jamie. Jamie has a seemingly unlimited credit card and is one of the most enthusiastic people I know. In a shop, Jamie will drape beautiful, glittery clothes on me and tell me I look amazing and I absolutely MUST buy that sequinned jumpsuit, no matter what it costs (or whether or not I will ever have the occasion to wear a sequinned jumpsuit). And it's all so fun that I can just never say no. So now I know that we just can't go shopping together, because I always end up buying things I will regret.

In your life, you will have friends who are richer than you, and friends who are poorer than you. You'll have friends who are better at managing their money, and friends who spend money like it's water. Learning how to draw boundaries with your friends is the way to make sure money doesn't get in the way of your friendship.

My friends and I like to use an app to keep track of shared costs like restaurant bills (two apps I like are called Splitwise and Kin). That makes it easier to have a system where one person gets the Uber and someone else buys the food, for instance, without things getting out of hand.

I don't believe in lending money to friends. I only believe in **giving** money, and only when you can afford to and truly want to. That's because I value friendship more than I value money, and lending money to friends can be the fastest way to lose both.

The moment you lend money to your friend, you are becoming their bank. This might introduce new feelings into your friendship that don't belong there: your friend might feel guilty if they can't pay you back right away; you might feel judgemental if you see your friend buying luxuries rather than paying you back immediately, or you might feel like your friend is taking advantage of you. Any of these feelings could strangle your friendship. It's just not worth it.

Appreciate what you have

One of the things we humans do is buy things to fill up the holes in our hearts. We hope buying things will make us more lovable or successful or envied. Adults are just as guilty of this as teens. The much better way to fix our hearts is just to actually work on feeling okay with who we are.

One of the techniques for doing this, which is backed up by mountains of scientific research, is so simple it seems silly: at the end of every day, write down three things you're grateful for.

Ja, I know, it's cheesy, but it works.

You already own a whole bunch of stuff. When you bought that stuff, you thought it would make you happier. So before you buy something new, spend some time caring for what you already own. Clean it, organise it. Be grateful for it. Before you buy new clothes, go through your closet and touch and put on all the clothes you already have. Before you buy new books, go through the books you already have and haven't read yet. Your life is already pretty great.

Break your habits

Think you're in control of your decisions? HAH! Half the time you're not even aware of the fact that you're making them.

Let me ask you a question: what did you do during the first hour you were awake yesterday morning? Did you have cereal for breakfast? Meet a group of friends on the way to class before first period? What about the day before that?

For 90% of our life, people are on autopilot. Our brains are responding to cues around us and executing habits like a machine. Some of these habits involve us mindlessly spending money on things that don't even make us happy.

Habits work in a little cycle:

- The cue – the trigger that makes your brain unconsciously crave the reward, like walking past the vending machine or seeing an ad from your favourite T-shirt brand.
- The habit – the action that you take.
- The reward – the dopamine kick you get from the sugar in your system, the quenching of your thirst, etc.

Don't even try to willpower your way out of a habit: it's too hard!

Rather try this. First, spend some time understanding what your own cue–habit–reward cycle looks like. Keep a journal for a few days. Every time you do the thing, note down where you were and how you were feeling before, during and after the thing. Try to ask yourself what reward you are actually craving – if you go get a donut every afternoon with your friend, maybe the reward is the time you're spending with the friend rather than the donut itself.

Once you understand your cue–habit–reward cycle, you have a couple of options:

- Avoid the cue, if it's something you can avoid.
- When the cue triggers you, replace the habit with a different habit that has a similar reward. For instance, instead of buying donuts with your friend, go for a short walk around the block with your friend, or go shoot some hoops.

Habits are deeply psychological, and you need some pretty profound soul-searching to tackle them. A few years ago, I realised that every few months I was going on a shopping spree and buying clothes I didn't need. When I spent time observing myself, I realised that I did this whenever I felt really unattractive – that was my cue.

The reward was feeling more in control of my body again, because I could make myself look nicer with kiff clothes. Instead of just trying to never feel unattractive, which is hard, I replaced the habit with stuff that gets me the same reward and is actually healthy: when I feel gross, I go do some exercise. Once you understand your triggers and the real emotional source of your cravings, switching your habits gets much easier.

Return stuff you don't want

Most shops will let you return goods, unused and in the original condition, if you return them before a certain date. Some shops will give you your cash back, others will give you a voucher to spend at the shops. This is not an invitation to buy things without thinking (or to use things and then return them – that's just scaly), but if you find out you regret a purchase, just take it back.

You don't need to feel awkward about returning stuff! If anything, maybe the SHOP should feel awkward for manipulating you into buying something you didn't actually want.

Make a habit of finding out the store policy on returns before you buy. And keep your receipts in a safe place.

> Practise returning something so that you can get over the embarrassment. Buy something (cheap) that you know you hate from a shop that offers cash returns. Take it back the next day. See, not so bad, was it?

Go back to cash

If you're struggling not to overspend on a bank card, go back to cash and paper envelopes. It will make it easier to control your spending, I promise.

Shop slooooooooowly

It can be helpful to imagine that you have two different brains inside your head. This is going to sound weird, but stay with me.

Your front-brain, let's call it, is a sophisticated guy. If that brain was a person, they'd be staying in doing crossword puzzles for fun or reading the dictionary. That brain is SMART.

Your other brain, though . . . that brain isn't smart, but it sure is EXCITED. If that brain was a person, they'd be running around like a five-year-old who's had too much sugar, giggling like a maniac and looking for fun. Let's call that your back-brain.

Now, it should be obvious that your front-brain generally makes better decisions than your back-brain. But there's one problem: your front-brain makes decisions really slooooowly, because it likes to weigh up all the options and think through every possible consequence of a choice. If you let your front-brain make all of your decisions, you would never get anything done. Which is why, in reality, it's your back-brain that makes decisions most of the time.

Your back-brain is a really important brain. It's the brain that reacts in a scary or dangerous situation where there's no time to think. The two brains have different strengths, and we need them both.[63] Your front-brain isn't **better** than your back-brain, but it IS the brain that makes better decisions about spending money.

The trick to letting your front-brain be the brain that's in charge of your spending is to buy stuff at your front-brain's pace: that is, as *slooooooowly* as possible. A **front-brain** shops like this:

- BEFORE it goes to the shops, it spends a few days thinking about exactly what it wants to buy, and what the criteria are for choosing the best product.
- BEFORE it goes to the shops, it reads reviews online (and it's careful to check that the reviews aren't adverts in disguise or celebrity endorsements).
- BEFORE it goes to the shops, it does some research to figure out how much it wants to spend (without falling for the *anchoring* of what stuff costs in one shop).
- THEN it goes to the shops, and checks the quality of the thing and the returns policy of the shop, and if the thing is exactly right, it buys it!

If you find yourself impulse shopping, grabbing something you see in the shop because it looks cool, that's your **back-brain** making the decision. Instead, try giving yourself a 'cooling-off' rule if you see something rad in a shop, where you have to wait at least 24 hours between seeing something

---

63 I know this analogy sounds odd, but people who study human behaviour say that we really do have two totally different ways of thinking. Scientists call it 'system 1 thinking' and 'system 2 thinking', and a guy called Daniel Kahneman won a Nobel Prize for explaining it.

you want and buying it. That gives your front-brain time to wake up, check out the situation, and intervene if there's something smarter you could be doing with that money.

When I was growing up, my mum and I had a cooling-off rule of three months after I started a new hobby, before I was allowed to buy the gear for that hobby. That's because I have a strong and powerful back-brain that gets extremely enthusiastic about signing up for things (Learning a new instrument! Martial arts! Yoga! Painting! YAYYYY!) but loses interest after about a month.

Look, I know this all sounds like a pretty boring way to live but it's especially important to let your front-brain take the lead on big money decisions. Do let your back-brain go shopping occasionally to let off steam, but only give it access to your Fun Money envelope.

Look for bargains

If you're shopping slowly and your front-brain is in control (that is, you've got a list and a budget, and you've already done research about what you want), then shopping at sales can be a great way to save money. Just remember that sales are bait for the back-brain, so don't go into a sale unless you've got a plan. *Never bring your back-brain to a sale!*

My favourite way to find bargains isn't at sales, it's by buying used stuff. I buy my tech, clothes, shoes, household stuff, most of it second-hand. It's a great way to find things that are unique and interesting. This is also much better for the environment: constantly making new things is ruining the planet we live on.

If it's tech you are into, just remember that the makers bring out new series and updates annually just to get you to buy new gadgets every year. Don't fall into this trap. Did technology really get that much better over the past year that your life will be more fulfilled if you have the best screen resolution?

Look at the total cost

One day, when you're looking at getting your first cellphone (or maybe you're lucky enough to have one already), you'll see that getting a cellphone contract looks much cheaper than buying a phone outright. But actually, this is just a way that marketers trick you.

You see, cellphone contracts are a weird form of debt, where you pay off a gadget over two years. The monthly payment amounts can look quite small, so you don't look at what the gadget costs you overall.

Most people, if they were looking at buying a new cellphone outright, would look at the R15 000 price tag and think, *Good grief, why would I spend that much money on a phone?!* If you wouldn't buy it outright, why on earth would you pay even more money for it over two years of your life?

So, if your parents have agreed to buy you a cellphone – or let you save up to buy one – then tell them you actually want to vasbyt. Save up and buy a phone with cash. You can get pretty cheap cellphones these days (take a look at the Chinese brands, or buy a second-hand Samsung/iPhone). Then, get a prepaid SIM card for it.

This is a good rule for everything in life, not just phones: don't get distracted looking at the monthly cost of a debt – look at the overall cost. It's almost always cheaper to save up and buy something with cash than to get into debt.

Remember this one day when you're ready to buy a car.

A little buys a lot of happiness

The daughter of a friend of mine really loves making music – she has been singing and writing songs since primary school. In Grade 10 she wanted to get herself a pretty expensive electronic keyboard. She'd saved up for it, so she was entitled to do that. But her choir teacher found out about it and suggested that rather than buying the keyboard she thought she needed, she get a much cheaper one. The teacher knew that for what she needed, the quality of the cheaper one was good enough. She also knew that if Marli blew all her savings on that keyboard, she'd be stuck with no spending money when the choir went on a music-appreciation trip to a music festival in Joburg. So Marli did just that, and she was able to use the difference in price to buy not only a couple of signed CDs from the local musicians on the trip, but also an online subscription to really nice recording and editing software – so now she's making her first music video.

The thing is, research has shown that people are generally more happy when they spend SMALL amounts of money MORE OFTEN on the things that cost LESS. Buying lots of small things makes you happier than buying one big thing.

So, if you're keeping a wish list of big things you want to buy, consider buying the cheaper version of those things so that you can buy other stuff too.

BEWARE OF SCHEMES AND SCAMS

South Africa's famous for two things these days: crime and Nando's. And I'm not here to tell you about Nando's.

When you open a bank account, the bank will give you some advice about security, which you should make sure you follow. If you have one already, you all already know the basics, like not to let anyone 'help' you at the ATM, and not to tell anyone your PIN (even if you're on the phone to someone who says they're calling from your bank). Try not to let anyone walk out of your sight with your bank card. And never throw papers in the bin that contain important information, like your bank statements (burn or shred them instead).

When you're banking online, remember these tips:

- Only use a secure, private network to do banking – don't do it at an internet café or on an unsecured network, like the hotspot at the mall.
- Make sure you are on the actual bank's website, and not a fake website, and that the website is secure (it should say 'HTTPS' in front of the address, not 'HTTP').
- Never save your banking passwords on any device.
- You'll also get real-time SMS or e-mail notifications of transactions as an extra level of security, and you need to check that these are correct.
- Never click on a link in an e-mail that takes you to your bank's website. Always type in the address. Scammers send out e-mails pretending they're from your bank, and try to get you to enter your password on a fake website (this is called phishing).
- Actually log out of your account when you are finished. Don't leave the web page open or just close the page.

If you're using a banking app:

- Firstly, make sure you don't download a fake app. Check the reviews on the app store.
- When you are logging in, it will also be a combination of two or three methods – username, password, PIN. Some cellphone banking apps are starting to use more

sophisticated methods, like fingerprints and voice recognition. Use these options if they're available.

* Log out properly when you are finished. Don't just close the app.
* Again, never save your banking password on your phone, or on a laptop.
* If you are going to bank on your phone, then make your phone secure. Make sure it has a login code, so that if it's lost or stolen it's more difficult for people to get into it to use the information.

For both internet and cellphone banking, be wary of public places, where people might see what you are typing into your device.

What to do when the fraudsters get you

Generally, if money is stolen from your bank account, banks are responsible for paying you back. (That's why we keep our money at the bank, after all.) Honestly, though, they'll often find some excuse not to pay you back. It sucks. Here's what to do when stuff goes wrong.

If money goes missing from your account:
1. Call your bank's fraud hotline immediately.
2. Try to get the bank to trace the fraudulent transaction(s).
3. Sometimes, the bank can refund you part or all of the amount that was stolen. You will need to submit a fraud claim form.
4. You should also open a case file with the police.

If your card gets stolen:
1. Call your bank's fraud hotline immediately.
2. Get them to block the card.

3. If your phone was stolen at the same time, try to wipe your phone remotely. Criminals can use information they find on your phone, with your card, to do more complicated fraud stuff.

4. Check the recent transactions on the card with the bank. The bank will try to stop them. If they have already been processed fully, you may be unable to get your money back.

If you've lost your card and you're not sure whether it's been stolen:

1. Sigh. One day, banks will let us put a temporary block on a card that can be reversed, so we don't feel like a fool if we later find our card in our jeans pocket or something. Right now, most banks don't.

2. Err on the side of caution, and block it as soon as you realise you can't find it.

If you find out that someone has opened an account in your name:

1. This is a form of identity theft. Treat this like a crime, including reporting it to the police.

2. If a parent or guardian has done this without your knowledge, and with the intention to defraud you, then involve a lawyer before you report it and get advice on how to handle the situation. Call the Legal Aid hotline – they can advise you for free.

3. Notify the institution that the account was opened fraudulently.

4. If you suspect that someone has a fraudulent or stolen copy of your ID document, report it to Home Affairs.

IN SUMMARY!

- Resist mind control by understanding the tricks that advertisers and marketers use, so you can spot when you're being manipulated.
- There are lots of tricks for being a savvier spender, but most of them boil down to understanding yourself, and spending money more slowly and thoughtfully (so your front-brain is making the big decisions).
- Stay safe from sneaky fraudsters!

Chapter 11

MONEY AS A FORCE FOR GOOD

You're going to have a lot of money to manage over your lifetime. That's a big responsibility, because money is powerful. You can use that power for good or for evil. Let's close this book by talking about some of the ways money can be used to do good in the world.

GIVING TO CHARITY

You know that the world is an unequal place. One of the simplest ways to do good with your money is to give it to people who need it more than you do, or to give it to organisations that are fighting to fix the world's biggest problems.

Here's the good news: giving to charity is as good for YOU as it is for the charity! Research shows that giving to charity is one of the types of spending that makes you the happiest. Giving money can also help you to feel less powerless about the issues that keep you up at night. You can know that you're actually doing something to help fix a problem.

Do your research about the charity you're donating to: sadly, some people do set up fake charities as a way to scam money out of good people. So make sure your charity money really is going to where you think it is going. I've got a list of registered charities online that you can use as a starting point. They cover charities that are doing all sorts of things like saving the environment, protecting animals, looking after orphaned children, caring for vulnerable people living with disabilities, helping to reduce disease, supporting LGBTI + people, doing investigative journalism to uncover corruption, or changing the laws to make society more equal. Some people choose to give through their religious institution, which can also be a great way to give money.

You might choose to just give money occasionally, or to set up a recurring payment every month (so that you think of charity as just being one of your envelopes).

Remember that you can give more than just money: you can give your time, too. Getting involved and volunteering for a charity organisation can be a great way to learn new things, connect with people, and be of service to the world. I promise you that you'll get as much out of it as you give.

TAXES

All of us pay a portion of our money to the government. This is called tax.

Taxes are important, because they're how we build roads and schools and hospitals. Sometimes taxes are misused by corrupt people, but no society can function without finding a way for people to invest in things everyone can benefit from, and taxes are the best way we've found to do that (so far).

Taxes can also help to make unequal countries more equal. Sweden is one of the most equal countries in the world, but a big part of that is because they tax the rich and give that money back to the poor. Without taxes, Sweden would be a less equal country. More equal countries have less violence and tend to be happier places for everyone.

There are a lot of different types of taxes you'll encounter in your life. Here are the important ones to know about:

VAT

This is the type of tax that you're paying already. Value-added tax (VAT) is tax built into the price of any goods or services that are sold. Some things also have other special taxes to encourage people to buy them or discourage them from buying them – like the 'sin tax' on soft drinks or cigarettes.

Personal income tax

Every person who earns more than a certain amount each year (about R80 000) has to pay some of it to the government. People with full-time jobs usually have theirs paid automatically by their employer before it hits their bank account (it's called PAYE, or 'pay as you earn' tax). You pay income tax regardless of the source of the income: a salaried job, side-hustles, selling things, renting out your house, all of it.

The year you earn your first real paycheque, you'll need to go and register at SARS: the South African Revenue Service, aka The Taxman. If you earn a decent amount of money, you need to complete a tax return every year to make sure that you've paid SARS the right amount.[64]

Income tax works on a sliding scale, so the more money you earn, the bigger a percentage you have to pay in taxes.

Capital gains tax and dividends tax

Capital gains tax is a tax you pay when assets you own increase in value. This usually only comes into play when you sell an asset. You also have to pay taxes when your assets pay dividends.

---

64 SARS starts counting a new year from 1 March each year, because no one wants to be doing their tax returns on New Year's Eve. That's what people mean when they talk about the 'tax year'.

Estate tax

This is the tax you pay when you die. This is one reason rich people set up trusts.

Complaining about taxes

South Africa's top tax rate is 45%. Did you know that in the UK and the US, the top tax bracket was over 90% for parts of the 1950s and 1960s? Just some perspective for when you hear adults moaning about how their taxes are too high.

BUY ETHICALLY

Every time you give money to a business, you're casting a vote for the type of world you want to live in. You can see your money as a reward that you are giving to businesses that have done something you like. So if you want to support businesses that make products that are environmentally friendly or treat their workers well or support your local community, buy their stuff.

You have a duty as someone with money to know about what kind of world you're voting for when you spend. That means taking the time to learn about your favourite brands and products. Where is your food grown? How are your clothes made? Who gets the profits from your new cellphone? You can find the answers to all of these questions online, and many of them may shock you.

Look, none of us can be perfect all the time. Usually, ethical stuff costs more than unethical stuff, because unethical companies just make their damage someone else's problem (an unethical company will just dump their waste products into the environment, for example). But do your best. This stuff matters.

You can be an ethical consumer when it comes to the businesses you buy pieces of, too (your shares). Don't want to give your money to companies that are contributing to global warming, making people sick or abusing animals? It's now possible to buy simple global index funds that exclude unethical companies. There aren't enough of these in South Africa yet, but new ones are launching every year.

> What was the last global company you bought something from? Spend ten minutes online researching that company. A good place to start is a website like rankabrand.org.

GET INVOLVED

It's not enough for all of us to make small changes in our everyday lives. To really make a difference, we need to change the big systems in society. We need to change laws. We need to start new types of businesses that make money without destroying the world or abusing people. We need to make sure that the people leading our governments are serving the nation, not themselves.

So, keep educating yourself about the stuff you care about. Tell other people about what you've learnt. Get involved in local politics. Become an activist. Use your unique skills and your talents as weapons in the fight for a better world.

None of this is easy, and none of us can do this alone. It's always been the young who've driven the biggest changes in society. And when I look at your generation, I'm filled with hope. I can't wait to see the kind of world you're going to build.

ENJOY YOUR LIFE

There is no rule book for how to live a happy life. Sometimes you have to do stuff that's pretty dumb, financially, because other things are more important. I once went into R100k worth of debt because I spent a year travelling overseas. I don't regret this debt, even though it set my money goals back by several years. I needed to do it, and I needed to do it at that time of my life.

Money is a part of life, for all of us. Money is power, and it's choice. It can trap you or it can liberate you.

The thing is, though, learning how to manage it better is something we'll all be doing throughout our whole lives. It's not like you figure it out and BAM, you get your 'I'm a Money Boss' trophy. There will be times when you mess up. But you're not trying to be perfect. You're trying to be better, and more conscious. You're trying to give yourself more options. You're trying to work towards a happier life that is more like the life you really want for yourself.

Most of this isn't about money at all. It's about knowing yourself. And getting wiser. And being mindful. And understanding what a meaningful life looks like, for you. It's about all of the strange twists and turns in the weird story that is your life.

So, actually, the best things you can do to be better with your money are to go on long walks in the mountains. Have long, honest talks deep into the night with your friends. Play board games with your family. Read. Practise a skill that makes you feel proud of yourself. Volunteer at an animal shelter. Make things. Learn to spend more time with yourself. Learn who you are. Learn what you actually care about, and don't let marketing mind-control ever distract you from those things.

You only get to live your life once. Enjoy it.

- **Asset:** Something you own that earns an income for you, or increases in value over time.
- **Balance sheet:** Where you keep track of all of your assets and debts.
- **Cash flow:** The total amount of money coming into your life and going out of your life. You want to have more money coming in than going out.
- **Compound interest:** When your interest also earns interest. This means that money can grow crazy-big over time.
- **Debt:** Money you owe to someone else. Sometimes called a liability.
- **Digby:** The world's dumbest cat.
- **Dividends:** When a company makes a profit, it can pay some of that profit to the people who own it (like people who've bought shares in that business).
- **Economic growth:** When a country becomes richer.
- **ETF (exchange-traded fund):** A bundle of shares that you can buy through the stock market.
- **Income:** Money you earn, either from doing a job or from owning things that make money (like leprechauns). It's called income because it's incoming money, get it? Money you get from working at a job is called *active income*, and money you get from owning stuff is called *passive income*.

- **Index tracker fund:** An easy way to buy a whole bunch of shares on a stock exchange in one go.
- **Inflation:** An increase in prices. Your money is worth less every year, because the cost of goods and services increases.
- **Inheritance:** When someone dies, they can choose to leave their money and other assets to someone else. That's called an inheritance.
- **Interest:** The cost of borrowing money from someone. You can also earn interest if you're the one lending the money, or by putting it in a savings account at the bank.
- **Investing:** Making money grow into more money by buying assets.
- **Marketing:** All the techniques businesses use to get people to buy their products or services, including advertising.
- **Net worth:** The difference between what your assets are worth and how much money you owe other people (your debts).
- **Raise:** A salary increase. Some people get a raise every year so that their salary keeps up with inflation. People can also get a raise when their boss thinks they're doing a good job, or when they get promoted.
- **Retirement:** When people stop working, usually because they're older than 65. Some people take 'early retirement' if they've saved enough money that they can afford to just live off their investments.
- **Royalties:** Money you get from other people who want to use something you own – like if you write a song, and someone else wants to use that song in their ad, they would pay you royalties.

- **Salary:** Money you earn from a full-time job, usually paid monthly. When people are paid weekly, that's usually called getting wages.
- **Shares (also called stocks or equities):** Pieces of a large business that are available to be bought or sold by the public.
- **Speculation:** Making guesses about whether things will go up in value or down, and making bets against other speculators who disagree, to make money.
- **Stock exchange:** A virtual marketplace where people buy and sell shares.
- **Trust:** A trust is like a company that manages assets, usually for very rich people.

BIBLIOGRAPHY

Andal, W. (2016). *Finance 101 for Kids: Money Lessons Children Cannot Afford to Miss*. Minneapolis: Mill City Press.

Booysen, W., Bronkhorst, J. & King, S. (2013). *Economic and Management Sciences: Learner's Book*. Cape Town: Oxford University Press.

Cruze, R. & Ramsey, D. (2014). *Smart Money, Smart Kids: Raising the Next Generation to Win with Money*. Brentwood: Lampo Press.

Cuban, M., Patel, S. & McCue, I. (2018). *Kid Start-up: How You Can Be an Entrepreneur*. New York: Diversion Books.

Dominguez, J. & Robin, V. (2008). *Your Money or Your Life*. London: Penguin Books.

Fisher-French, M. (2015). *Maya on Money: Implement Your Money Plan*. Cape Town: Tafelberg.

Fontaine, M., Glista, J. & McKenna, J. (2016). *How to Turn $100 into $1,000,000: A Guide to Earning, Saving and Investing*. New York: Workman Publishing Company.

Honig, D. & Karlitz, G. (1999). *Growing Money: A Complete Investing Guide for Kids*. New York: Penguin Group.

Ingram, W. (2013). *Become Your Own Financial Advisor: The Real Secrets to Becoming Financially Independent*. Cape Town: Zebra Press.

Kahneman, D. (2011). *Thinking, Fast and Slow*. New York: Farrar, Straus and Giroux.

Kobliner, B. (2017). *Make Your Kid a Money Genius (Even if You're Not)*. New York: Simon & Schuster.

Pivnick, R. (2011). *What All Kids (and Adults Too) Should Know About Saving & Investing.* U.S.A.: CreateSpace Independent Publishing Platform.

ACKNOWLEDGEMENTS

First and foremost, thank you to Angela Briggs (and her dalmatian, Boogle), who helped me write this book. Many of its best ideas are hers, and it wouldn't have existed without her countless hours of hard work.

Thanks also to Jeremy Boraine for giving me the push I needed to get this done, and to Caren van Houwelingen, Jean-Marie Korff, Jennifer Ball, Nkanyezi Tshabalala, Elmarie Stodart and everyone else at Jonathan Ball who've midwifed this baby out into the world. Thank you also to Ester Levinrad, who got this whole party started in the first place.

Thanks to Angela Voges for tightening up the text and being patient with my overexcited! perpetual! use! of! exclamation! marks!

An overflowing barrel of gratitude to Nanna Venter, friend and favourite pencil-witch, who brought this book to life with her charming illustrations, and who also reminded me to 'shut up and write'.

League of Grownups, thank you for giving me the support and motivation I needed to keep doing this work. A special shout-out to Valen van Heerden and his extremely bodacious Grade 8s, 9s and 10s, who gave me insight into the big (and very poignant) questions young people are asking about money.

Charne Lavery, Meghan Finn, Dale Halvorsen, Shen Tian and Georgina Armstrong, I love you all and I owe you more than I can say. Gang of reprobates, you're weirdos and I miss you all, every day.

A particular nod to my friends Zani Muller, Jon Hodgson and Melanie Smuts, who've dedicated their lives to helping more kids in South Africa get the education that they deserve. I am astounded, every day, by the work you do and the people you are.

Simon Dingle and Kenny Inggs, thank you for having my back through even my most preposterous schemes and making it possible for me to live the life that I want to live.

Lauren Beukes, thank you for bringing me to life in a way I didn't know was possible, and to heck with you for being right all the time. You are the tiger-queen of my burning heart. And also a dork.

Thank you to all the kiddos and teens in my life, especially Keitu, Zoe, Dom, Ronan, Gabriel and Cian, for being so delightfully weird and fun to hang out with, and for being the reason I wanted to write this book. Keitu, an extra thank you for being my first reader and pointing out where I was being boring (and thank you for not suggesting that I turn the whole book into a book about horse facts). Thank you also to Gaby and Jordan, who are now EXTREMELY GROWN UP, but still delightfully weird. I adore you all.

Matty P, you are the other half of my space team and anywhere is home if we're there together. I can't wait to explore this whole dumb galaxy with you.

Mum, I have loved you every second of my life. Dyl, I'm running around you in circles. Whatcha gonna do about it? Huh? Huh?!

Finally, Digby, you can't even read so I don't know why I'm thanking you here, but you fill every day with joy and it's stupid how obsessed with you I am. Thanks for infecting me with your toxoplasmosis. I love you always.

www.ingramcontent.com/pod-product-compliance
Lightning Source LLC
Chambersburg PA
CBHW071546200326
41519CB00021BB/6638